Shaw
on
Dickens

To Three Ellens:
Two Past And One Present

Shaw
on
Dickens

Edited With an Introduction by
Dan H. Laurence and Martin Quinn

Frederick Ungar Publishing Co.
NEW YORK

Library of Congress Cataloging in Publication Data

Shaw, Bernard, 1856–1950.
  Shaw on Dickens.

  Includes index.
  1. Dickens, Charles, 1812–1870—Criticism and interpretation—Addresses, essays, lectures. 2. Dickens, Charles, 1812–1870—Influence—Shaw—Addresses, essays, lectures. 3. Shaw, Bernard, 1856–1950—Knowledge—Literature—Addresses, essays, lectures. I. Laurence, Dan H., 1920– II. Quinn, Martin, 1945– . III. Title.
PR4588.S37   1984   823'.8   82-40257
ISBN 0-8044-2494-2

Contents

PART III

Dickensian Shavings

Introduction

"Now it is pretty clear," Bernard Shaw wrote when he was nearly thirty-seven, "that Dickens, having caught me young when he was working with his deepest intensity of conviction, must have left his mark on me."[1] Archibald Henderson confirms that "at the age of seven Sonny eagerly devoured the tense dramas of *Great Expectations* and *A Tale of Two Cities*," and—by the time he was thirteen—*Pickwick Papers* and two of the darker novels, *Bleak House* and *Little Dorrit*.[2] Ample evidence exists that Shaw's identification with Charles Dickens was thorough and that his sense of affection, rising even to hero worship, was vast. Moreover, this enthusiasm would exert an early and profound impact on Shaw's art. When he first read *Great Expectations*—mentioned so frequently as to suggest that it was his favorite Dickens novel—Shaw was, he related in an 1893 music review, "not much older than Pip was when the convict turned him upside down in the churchyard."[3]

Dickens's burgeoning works were themselves frequently turned upside down, if not inside out, by Shaw as budding novelist and later as celebrated playwright perennially in search of characters, situations, and conversations to illustrate an evolving philosophy. As he determined to win a reputation by his pen, Shaw perceived Dickens as a kindred genius who had filled his own childhood imagination and directed the first quickenings of his social conscience. As the Dickensian Walter Crotch observed in 1919: "[I]n temperament they were alike, in that both of them were intensely earnest, intensely vitalised, and intensely pugnacious. There was no subject on which they had not views that they did not rush to express—usually, both of them with the force and point that comes from originality of belief; there was no current controversy in which they did not take part."[4] Dickens became the most dramatic of novelists in an era when theater, committed almost wholly to melodrama and spectacle, was scarcely an admissible vocation. Shaw found himself the most prolific and forensic of modern playwrights in an age when the new drama had become not only respectable but simultaneously relevant, serious, and subversive. Both were irrepressibly egotistical writers, addicted to their roles as public personalities and entertainers. One crashed headlong into success in the flush of youth while the other labored in comparative obscurity until near middle age. The triumph of "Boz" had been edged in tragedy and cut short by early death, while the devil's Celtic disciple in serene old age threatened to survive his own legend. Of Dickens's great influence upon him, Shaw flamboyantly pronounced the challenge: "Nothing but the stupendous illiteracy of modern criticism could have missed this fact."[5]

However deep he may have been touched, Shaw was to write no extended work about Charles Dickens as he had written about Henrik Ibsen in *The Quintessence of Ibsenism* (1891), and about another of his well-advertised heroes, Richard Wagner, in *The Perfect Wagnerite* (1898). Nevertheless, that his enthusiasm for Dickens must have considerably antedated his attraction to the Norwegian playwright and the German composer, to both of whom he devoted book-length studies, is reflected in an incomplete essay entitled "From Dickens to Ibsen," a draft Shaw began in November 1889. The fragment, subsequently abandoned, is reproduced here for the first time; the surviving twenty-two manuscript pages are all on Dickens. Shaw presumably dropped the project after he had finished what he wanted to say about Dickens but before he could collect his thoughts for whatever was intended to follow. Indeed, he had already absorbed Dickens rather efficiently through five apprentice novels, written, he liked to claim, in the style of Dickens and Scott. While Shaw sprinkled everything he wrote, including his plays, with allusions to Dickens's stories and characters, his major statements were to await invitations in 1911 and in 1936 to write introductions for editions of *Hard Times* and *Great Expectations*.

Although their lifetimes overlapped for nearly fourteen years, Shaw reported in answer to a February 1912 *Bookman* questionnaire that he had no personal recollections of Dickens,[6] who had given his second series of public readings from the novels in a Fenian-plagued Ireland at Dublin and Belfast in early 1867.[7] Nevertheless, Blanche Patch, Shaw's confidential secretary for thirty years, was guilty of perpetuating a colossal misunderstanding and a rash of troubled queries to *The Dickensian*, house organ of the Dickens Fellowship, when in a ghost-written memoir published after her employer's death she claimed that "Shaw himself had met Charles Dickens . . . [who] had shown him a different ending to *Great Expectations*."[8] Since Dickens died in June 1870, before Shaw was quite through adolescence or had yet gone to England, this strange, charming legend remains just that. Yet, as in myth generally, an element of truth lurks: Shaw *did* know about the original discarded ending of the novel before most readers, and in 1936 took pains to see it restored, almost as an act of revisionist filial piety to his master. Perhaps the most significant fact, however, is that Shaw's familiarity with Dickens was so intense and obvious that a long-time associate received the impression that the two had been friends.[9]

Actually, Bernard Shaw and Charles Dickens emerged from rather different backgrounds, with Shaw holding the edge on social and cultural advantages. While Shaw's antecedents sprung from well-connected Irish Protestants, Dickens's paternal grandparents were life-long servants. Nevertheless, the parents of both spent most of their lives skirting the fringes of shabby-gentility, never achieving success, though always looking, Micawber-like, for the fresh opportunity. Perhaps more significant psychologically, Shaw and Dickens shared as children remarkably similar embarrassments in a sudden loss of social status—a factor which in itself may have drawn "Sonny" Shaw to the adventures of those castaway boys, Oliver Twist, David Copperfield, and Pip.

Dickens suffered lifelong pangs from the shameful experience of the blacking factory to which he was consigned following his father's imprisonment for debt. Edgar Johnson relates how John Dickens held a respectable position as a clerk in the Navy Pay Office, so that the family was even able to maintain a servant, until his arrest and the confiscation of the family belongings dashed his young son's expectations. The account of Dickens's containment of disgrace is familiar: "I never said, to man or boy, how it was that I came to be there, or gave the least indication of being sorry that I was there. That I suffered in secret, and that I suffered exquisitely, no one ever knew but I." Deeply wounded by his lost expectations, the boy Dickens would walk after work to the doorstep of an imposing house, in an effort to delude fellow factory hands concerning his real circumstances. Years later, successful and secure beyond question, he habitually avoided Hungerford Stairs, crossing to the other side of the street when he smelled the cement of the blacking corks coming from Robert Warren's blacking factory in the Strand.[10]

For Shaw the months as a student in the Dublin Central Model School among mainly working-class Catholic boys during a spell of family hard times was the painful "Secret Kept for 80 Years," published under the title "Shame and Wounded Snobbery" in *Sixteen Self Sketches*, 1949. Shaw described his adjustment to reduced status in terms that are like nothing so much as an unmasking of Dickens's reaction to the blacking factory: "There I was a superior being, and in play hour did not play, but walked up and down with the teachers in their reserved promenade."[11] B. C. Rosset, in *Shaw of Dublin* (1964), suggests that Shaw concocted this Dickens-like experience to cover his real anxiety about his paternity in an effort to throw inquisitive biographers off the true scent as to the identity of his father: George Carr Shaw, the alcoholic ne'er-do-well married to his mother, or George John (Vandeleur) Lee, the talented musician whose house the Shaw family shared in Dublin and who led the mother's, daughter's, and eventually son's hegira to London. This circumstance, according to Rosset, might have encouraged young Shaw to empathize with Dickens's orphans, and, moreover, could account for the number of occasions in which Shaw introduces foundlings and an element of doubtful paternity into his plays and novels, as in *Cashel Byron's Profession, Mrs Warren's Profession, Major Barbara, Misalliance,* and *The Fascinating Foundling*.[12] Rosset's ingenious thesis notwithstanding, anyone familiar with theater would immediately recognize that Shaw was drawing upon a tradition as venerable as *Oedipus Rex* and as modern as Wilde's *The Importance of Being Earnest*, employed as frequently by Gilbert and Sullivan in fourteen comic operas as by Shaw in his extended canon of fifty-one plays and five novels.

Dickens, of course, drew heavily on his bitter memory in *David Copperfield*, but Shaw felt the compensatory necessity to acquire a philosophy rather than, as he put it, to "bombinat[e] in vacuo." "We have," he wrote to H. G. Wells, whom he once described as Dickens's successor, "all been throug[h] the Dickens blacking factory; and we are all socialists by reaction against that; but the world wants from men of genius what they have divined as well as what they have gone through."[13] Accordingly, Shaw's sharpest criticism of Dickens was finally that he was an artist who suffered without achieving a productive philosophy.

Perhaps as important as Shaw's supposedly suppressed concern for his legitimacy was the unquestioned fact of his unhappy upbringing and a sense of remoteness from a mother forever pursuing her own ambitions, albeit never fulfilled. The "Parents and Children" preface to *Misalliance*, in which the notion of consanguinity engendering revulsion is introduced, was an indictment from the depth of his being; the document, moreover, is filled with references to Dickens. "The very people," Shaw writes, "who read with indignation of Squeers and Creakle in the novels of Dickens are quite ready to hand over their own children to Squeers and Creakle, and to pretend that Squeers and Creakle are monsters of the past."[14] His theory, "as you may have noticed in my books here and there," he told Gilbert Murray in 1911, "is that blood relationship tends to create repugnance, and that family affection is factitious."[15] Yet, as if to admit that he knew the pangs of something more than familial ambivalence, he wrote to Ellen Terry of his life as a boy: "Oh, a devil of a childhood, Ellen, rich only in dreams, frightful and loveless in realities."[16] In his ninth decade Shaw confided almost enviously to Esmé Percy, "You are very lucky to have such a nice mother [the mother in question was ill]. Look at the awful mothers most people have."[17]

Dickens's biographer John Forster reported that even after his deliverance Dickens never pardoned his mother for her willingness to keep him working at the hated warehouse: "I never afterwards forgot, I never shall forget, I never can forget, that my mother was warm for my being sent back."[18] Thus, we have in Dickens's works typically two kinds of mothers: the ideal, angelic, and— significantly—dead mothers of Oliver, David, and Pip and the more sharply visualized, believable, remote and Puritanical "mother" of Arthur Clennam in *Little Dorrit*, a work Shaw insisted was Dickens's real autobiography. Actually, Mrs Clennam is not the hero's biological parent since Arthur, we learn, is the product of an extramarital by-blow.

Similarly, the parade of unsympathetic and/or ineffectual mothers in Shaw's works—notably Adelaide Gisborne, Mrs. Warren, Mrs. Clandon, Mrs. Dudgeon, Mrs. Whitefield, Lady Britomart, Mrs. Knox, Mrs. Tarleton, Mrs. Higgins, and Mrs. Mopply—is formidable. The very names "Britomart" and "Dudgeon" are evocative of character. Mrs. Dudgeon, Shaw confessed, was but "a replica of Mrs. Clennam with certain circumstantial variations, and perhaps a touch of the same author's Mrs. Gargery [Pip's shrewish sister and surrogate mother] in *Great Expectations*."[19] The play in which Mrs. Dudgeon appears, *The Devil's Disciple*, was, moreover, clearly "written round the scene of Dick's arrest,"[20] which Shaw knew could not help but remind audiences of Sydney Carton's ultimate predicament in *A Tale of Two Cities*.

Saturated as he was with Dickens and keenly aware of embarrassments in his family background, Shaw sensed, not surprisingly, an extension of George Carr's spirit in John Dickens, the father of the novelist, on whom Dickens's portraits of Wilkins Micawber and, later, William Dorrit were principally modeled. Dubbed "The Hermit" by his offspring and their friends, George Carr Shaw became increasingly unresponsive to his children as he lapsed into ever more profound bouts of depression and dipsomania. It was natural and inevitable that young Sonny should turn to the sympathetic and considerate Lee, from whom he received encouragement in art and music, and remain on friendly terms with the "Professor" long after his mother and sister had dropped him. Charles MacMahon Shaw, an Australian cousin of G. B. S., wrote that he could not "help feeling that Mr. Micawber is probably far more like G. B. S.'s father than is G. B. S.'s own sketch [in the preface to *Immaturity*]." "Like John Dickens," C. M. Shaw recalled, "he began in a Government office, and what could be more optimistically Micawberish than Uncle George's venture into the corn trade, about which he knew nothing whatever?"[21] Like Dickens in his portrait of Micawber—and through Freudian impulses—Shaw may, cousin Charles suggests, have "struck at his father to protect his own ego." Thus Shaw's famous remark about clinging at an advanced age to his father's coattails and hurling his mother into the struggle for life may be interpreted as bravura utterances designed to conceal a painful reality. In fact, rather like Dickens's waifs, no one in his family cared much about him.

In essence Sonny Shaw—a lonely, sensitive, unloved boy, as isolated himself as "The Hermit"—moved into Dickens's world of castaway youngsters who generally managed ultimately to find safe havens, in Daniel Peggotty's converted boathouse (a motif Shaw uses as late as *Heartbreak House* in Captain Shotover's drawing room got up like the poop deck of a ship), in Solomon Gills's snug Wooden Midshipman, or even ultimate legitimacy as the adopted son of the benevolent gentleman Mr. Brownlow. (Consider the parallel relationship of Adolphus Cusins and Andrew Undershaft in *Major Barbara*.) Thus, the child acquired a whole set of fictional relatives and warm associations that seeped into his consciousnesss and stayed with him all his life—to emerge demonstratively in his creative works and as metaphor in his very language.

And while children as characters do not figure in his plays,[22] the Dickensian legacy is that Shaw understood children and was to a rare degree sensitive to their peculiar angle of vision. Typically, he treated children as if they were adults—and thus his equals—often developing a special avuncular-fraternal affinity with the offspring of close friends. Tom Archer, son of the critic William Archer, admitted G. B. S. alone into his imaginary, mystical land of plenty, the world he called "Piona."[23]

Childhood trauma aside, there are several other inescapable biographical parallels between Shaw and Dickens that strengthen the affinity. Both began their writing careers in journalism, Dickens as a shorthand Parliamentary reporter, Shaw as a part-time art, music, and—finally—drama critic. Both outgrew the workaday expository medium, yet neither entirely forsook it for the more durable crafts of fiction and drama. With a mind perhaps as much on Dickens as on efficiency, Shaw even took the trouble to acquire and master Pitman shorthand, which he employed in diaries, correspondence, and drafts of many of his plays. Long after he was established as a playwright, G. B. S. continued to contribute to *The*

Nation, the *Labour Leader*, the *New Statesman*, and numerous newspapers of varying political persuasion in Britain and the United States. And, of course, he continued to coax the world to sanity in his lengthy prefaces. Similarly, Dickens wrote for many of the leading magazines of his day and, having secured an unsurpassed reputation as a novelist, conducted for the last twenty years of his life first *Household Words*, then *All the Year Round*, while simultaneously producing the later novels that Shaw and very few others of his generation recognized as major achievements.

Both Shaw and Dickens labored at first in the shadows of musically-talented elder sisters, singers with modest reputations that their brothers eventually eclipsed. Dickens's sister, Fanny (Frances Elizabeth Dickens Burnett), won a scholarship and actually took a prize at the Royal Academy of Music while Charles was still pasting labels on ink bottles. Her talent had blossomed early and she embarked on a promising musical career. Shaw's sister Lucy's entrancing voice similarly received recognition while her brother earned only frustration and a fluid prose style as a self-employed "novelist." Although her professional efforts are somewhat better known than those of Dickens's Fanny, Lucy never got beyond brief musical-theater success to achieve the prima-donna celebrity for which she longed.

While one hesitates to ride the horse of Plutarchian parallels too far, both brothers survived their sisters by more than twenty years as, unhappily, both Lucy and Fanny had their singing careers cut short by tuberculosis. The reactions of Shaw and Dickens to their sisters' final moments suggest nothing so much as very different responses to, or instincts about, the meaning of life. Or, as Hugh Kingsmill notes, "The chief and immense difference between them was in intensity of feeling,"[24] with the advantage falling to Dickens.

At Fanny's bedside, with an infallible eye for theatrical pathos, Dickens wrote his wife: "'No words can express the terrible aspect of suffering and suffocation—the appalling noise in her throat—and the agonizing look around,' followed repeatedly by a lethargy of exhaustion. 'Sleep seems quite gone, until the time arrives for waking no more.'"[25] Shaw in a very different tone dramatized the death of Lucy with ruthless objectivity, in cool, almost clinical, restrained, yet self-conscious, language containing barely a hint of sympathy:

One afternoon, when her health was giving some special anxiety, I called at her house and found her in bed. When I had sat with her a little while she said: "I am dying." I took her hand to encourage her and said, rather conventionally, "Oh, no: you will be all right presently." We were silent then; and there was no sound except from somebody playing the piano in the nearest house (it was a fine evening and all the windows were open) until there was a very faint flutter in her throat. She was still holding my hand. Then her thumb straightened. She was dead.[26]

In stoic dignity Shaw exhibited the philosophical response that his hero Dickens conspicuously lacked. His calm, unemotive reaction to mortality is the perfect antithesis to Dickens's sentimental, effusive rhetoric. The contrast is interesting not so much as a stylistic distinction (especially since Dickens is not seen here at his best), but rather as an indication of different apprehensions of reality and habits of perception.

Like many in turn-of-the-century London, Shaw *was* intimate with people who remembered Dickens in the flesh. Some, indeed, had sat at the table with the Dickens family, and through their eyes Shaw could attain to what Henry James called "the visitable past." Since he had read John Forster's book and was well acquainted with Dickens's pastimes, including an enthusiasm for tramping great distances through the city and the countryside, Shaw could refer casually to Dickens (and Meredith) "desperately taking long walks, like postmen," to relieve the strain of brainwork.[27] Moreover, he was apparently as inquisitive as most of literary London about the liaison with actress Ellen Ternan (who, he divined, must have been the model for Pip's Estella) and was aware of the cloud of personal scandal under which Dickens, after casting off his wife, spent his last and in many respects most miserable decade. G. B. S.'s own philanderings with actresses may even have been held in check by his knowledge of Dickens's bitter experience as well as by his vested interest in philosophic stability.

In 1885 Shaw—through the agency of William Archer—landed his first job as art (and, later, as music) critic on *The World*, then under the direction of Edmund Yates.[28] Son of Dickens's old actor-friend Frederick Yates and a frequent contributor in earlier days to *Household Words*, Edmund Yates first met Dickens in the spring of 1854. Yates had been intimate with Dickens, advising against publishing his "personal" statement on his separation from Mrs. Dickens and later embroiling the novelist in a feud with Thackeray that continued until just the week before Thackeray's death. Yates, however, would likely have done little to indulge Shaw's curiosity about Dickens's personal life since a year earlier he had put the public on notice that "My intimacy with Dickens, his kindness to me, my devotion to him, were such that my lips are sealed and my tongue is paralyzed as regards circumstances which, if I felt less responsibility and delicacy, I might be at liberty to state."[29]

Yet gossip flowed freely when Shaw asked the poet Richard Hengist Horne, who knew the Dickens household, what he thought of their domestic relations. R. H. Horne, who in 1852 became Commissioner for Crown Lands in Australia, had been a reporter on the ill-fated *Daily News* and a contributing editor to *Household Words*, as well as a sometime habitué of the Dickens party during holidays at Broadstairs. Consistent with a well-earned reputation as a colorful, flamboyant journalist, Horne related to Shaw Dickens's delight in mocking his wife's clumsiness, throwing "himself back in his chair . . . , his eyes streaming with mirth," utterly unable "to restrain his fits of laughter when Mrs. Dickens's bangles dropped from her fat little arms into the soup."[30] Shaw cautiously concluded that "Mrs. Dickens may have suffered from a want of respect in her humorous family, especially as the household was run and ruled by her sister Georgina."[31] Undoubtedly, Shaw's own evaluation of the conflicts in Dickens's life was partly shaped by this revealing conversation with Horne and by other testimony concerning the less flattering habits of the Victorian Household Saint.

Though the paths of Shaw and Dickens, Blanche Patch's fantasy notwithstanding, regrettably did not meet, for at least the last third of her long life (1839—1929) Shaw was a friend—if not precisely an intimate—of twice-married Kate Macready Dickens Collins Perugini, Dickens's third child and younger daughter (named both for her mother, Catherine, and the great actor and family friend William Charles Macready). Shaw's first encounter with Kate, fifteen years his senior, who had established herself as a painter of children's portraits and scenes from the nursery, seems to have occurred after he had severely criticized her paintings on display at the Royal Academy, complaining in *The World* that her pictures always told stories. As the widow of a member of the Pre-

Raphaelite Brotherhood (Charles Allston Collins, brother of Wilkie) and the wife of a wellknown Italian painter, Kate had reason to be proud.[32] Shaw's condescension apparently so infuriated Mrs. Perugini that she dashed off a bitter reply, which she almost instantly wished to recall. Sometime later they met at the Mansion House, where Shaw, ever playing the gallant, introduced himself to the distressed lady. Kate's wounded pride was soon assuaged, and her critic began sending inscribed copies of his latest works. On one occasion G. B. S. presented her with a picture postcard of himself that she dutifully exhibited on her mantelpiece next to a photograph of a friend's chauffeur's fiancée—fitting revenge upon a man Kate once sarcastically referred to as "Shernard Bore."[33]

While it must be emphasized that Shaw's friendship with Mrs. Perugini was purely incidental to his already profound involvement with Dickens's fiction, the relationship proved responsible for the rescue of a cache of 137 letters that Dickens had written to Catherine Hogarth before and long after their marriage. These letters, spanning the period 1835–1867, have since demonstrated their value to scholars and especially to Edgar Johnson, the heaven-sent biographer into whose hands Shaw hoped such documents might fall. The story of the letters is confusing, but it seems that a year before her death in 1879 the misused Mrs. Dickens entrusted the packet of correspondence to her eldest daughter, Mamie, asking only that their contents might one day be published. On Mamey's death in 1896 the burden of the letters fell upon Kate Perugini. "They would show the world, she [Mrs. Dickens] said, that my father had once loved her; and would make it apparent that the separation which took place between them in 1858, was not owing to any fault on her side,"[34] as Dickens had publicly and ungenerously suggested. Fiery-tempered Kate, "Lucifer Box" as her father dubbed her,[35] indignant about the treatment her mother had endured and probably suffering some guilt for the years that she had neglected her mother (in accord with what she supposed were Dickens's own wishes), was on the verge of committing the package to the fire when G. B. S. intervened.[36] As Shaw tells it, he opened her eyes "to the fact that there was a case for her mother as well as for her father" in what the letters might reveal.[37]

With urging from Shaw, Mrs. Perugini eventually changed her mind and agreed to deposit the letters in a sealed packet in the British Museum, with the stipulation that they not be made public until she and her surviving brothers, Sir Henry Fielding Dickens and Alfred Tennyson Dickens, could no longer be touched by their contents. After Henry's death in December 1933, the letters were finally made available to the public under the title *Mr. & Mrs. Charles Dickens.*[38] Ironically, without Shaw's timely persuasion, fewer of "those tragic monuments of dumbness of soul and noisiness of pen,"[39] as he later styled the correspondence of Charles Dickens to his family, would exist. This caustic remark in one of his own letters to the dean of Dickensians, G. K. Chesterton, was not the first disparaging reflection that Shaw made on his hero's human shortcomings, nor was it his last.

Forty years after Shaw rescued the Dickens letters from oblivion, and not long after the letters themselves were printed, the publication of two biographies stirred a vituperative squabble between defenders of Dickens's public reputation (marshaled under the banner of the Dickens Fellowship) and a few revisionists, including Shaw, who insisted on knowing even the unpleasant facts of Dickens's life. The two works that sparked this controversy were Thomas Wright's *The Life of Charles Dickens*[40] and Gladys Storey's overly-feared exposé, published four years later, *Dickens and Daughter.*[41] The daughter in the title was Kate Perugini, while the book itself is based on conversations with Mrs. Perugini, in lonely old age in her Chelsea flat confiding ambivalent feelings about her father.

Dickensians who still saw the novelist as the patron spirit of the English fireside stubbornly refused to accept the revelations about Dickens's character that seemed all at once to be coming to light, and suggested that Kate Perugini had gone senile. Public loyalty to lady friends was a chivalrous habit with Shaw; and indifferent to the purity of Dickens's posthumous image, he attested to the continuing soundness of Mrs. Perugini's judgment on the basis of a conversation shortly before her death. G. B. S. professed to have "no doubt that Miss Storey has carried out the wishes, early and late, of Mrs. Perugini in publishing her work." To the reviewer of *Dickens and Daughter* in the *Times Literary Supplement* who had entertained his readers with conjectures about the daughter's sanity, Shaw shot back an answer with solemn determination: "The facts of the case may be in bad taste. Facts often are. But either way your reviewer will be glad to have them put right."[42] The irony is that, like her mother and namesake, the other woman whose suffering eventually proved an embarrassment to Dickens's popularity, Kate's death was attended by murmurs of insanity.

Considering Shaw's long friendship with Mrs. Perugini, one is puzzled by the 1937 preface to *Great Expectations* in which Shaw disingenuously claimed to know *nothing* of the late phase of Dickens's career after the separation from his wife. Perhaps for "nothing" one can read "nothing for certain." In any case, Shaw simply assumed that at this time of his life Dickens was "free to make more intimate acquaintances with women than a domesticated man can."[43] To G. B. S., steering an uncharacteristic middle course, the argument sparked by the fanaticism of "the little sect of anti-Dickensites" and "provoked by the Dickens Fellowships" threatened to become as injurious and epidemic as the bickering over whether Francis Bacon wrote Shakespeare's plays. In a letter to Edith Nesbit Bland he had playfully suggested that Sidney Webb actually had written his own plays since "Shaw was an utterly ignorant man," descended from a ne'er-do-well father "just like old Shakespear or John Dickens."[44] This advertised affinity with Shakespeare and—for our purposes—Dickens must be recognized as something more than an idle remark.

It is clear, then, that Shaw was jolted by Dickens's fiction in his youth and absorbed into the fertile world of Dickens's imagination, where he identified with the novelist no less than with his castaway heroes. By chance or design Shaw also found himself drawn into the complicated affairs of Dickens's family in later life, proving his loyalty as an adviser and sometime advocate. Complaining once of having to stand out of the way of Dickens's novels to avoid wasting his time, Shaw was paying perverse tribute to the strength of what was for him a genuine literary passion.

ii

Shaw's enthusiasm for Dickens has been for some readers a source of amazement. J. B. Priestley, commenting on the seemingly futile attempt by Shaw and others to enlist Dickens in a particular cause or party (to make Boz, for instance, a proto-Marxist), discovers "a world of difference between the outlook of Shaw and the outlook of Dickens." Dickens, according to Priestley, wanted "to make the poor happy," while Shaw would apparently have preferred to turn them all into sensible "members of the Circumlocution Office,"[45] a conclusion reached perhaps by a too aggressive reading of *Major Barbara*. Edmund Wilson observes that Shaw's Dickens offset the confident Chestertonian interpretation "by praising the later and gloomier Dickens and insisting on his [Shaw's] own debt to the author of *Little Dorrit* at a time when it was taken for granted that he must derive from such foreigners as Ibsen and Nietzsche."[46] Placing Shaw among the defenders of Dickens, George Ford wrote: "Shaw's Dickens is certainly not the complete Dickens—if the complete Dickens does exist anywhere in criticism . . . his hug is hugely affectionate but so powerful that the object of his affections is squeezed out of shape." While the rotund G. K. Chesterton gave the world a Dickens stuffed "out of shape by overfeeding," Shaw applies so much of the opposite pressure that his effort delivers, according to Ford, "the thin man's Dickens."[47]

It may be further than thought can reach to imagine G. B. S. as simultaneously killjoy, pioneer illuminator, and asthenic fondler. However, Shaw's prefaces, letters, music, dramatic, and literary criticism are so crowded with capsule appraisals of Dickens's art as to lead critics to draw any number of contradictory conclusions. Always at Shaw's elbow, Dickens entered his creative imagination and became a subject for instant, continual reevaluation and metamorphosis.

Shaw typically refers to Dickens as a great genius. In an 1890s music review Dickens and Mozart are compared as the last of their breed; that is to say, each did all that could be done with the art form received from his predecessors. Shaw argues that "in art the highest success is to be the last of your race, not the first. Anybody, almost, can make a beginning: the difficulty is to make an end—to do what cannot be bettered." In his projection of the principles of Creative Evolution into an aesthetic judgment, Shaw finds perfection of form the ultimate achievement:

> For instance, if the beginner were to be ranked above the consum-
> mator, we should, in literary fiction, have to place Captain Mayne
> Reid, who certainly struck a new vein, above Dickens, who simply

took the novel as he found it, and achieved the feat of compelling his successor (whoever he may be), either to create quite another sort of novel, or else to fall behind his predecessor as at best a superfluous imitator.[48]

Yet, when pushed to defend Ibsen, Wagner, and Meredith, Shaw reverses his stance by emphasizing originality. If Ibsen, Wagner, and Meredith had the "astonishing specific talent" of Dickens and Mozart, Shaw suggests, they would hardly have been innovators:

All art is gratuitous; and the will to produce it, like the will to live, must be held to justify itself. When that will is associated with brilliant specific talent for the established forms and attractions of fine art, no advance is made, because the artist can distinguish and satisfy himself by novel, witty, and touching rehandlings of the old themes.[49]

Sensing the truth in both pronouncements, anyone following the argument might feel bewildered by the paradox. Resolution, however, is not to be found in logical analysis but in Shaw's perception of Dickens. The early Dickens, still adhering to the traditions of the eighteenth-century novel, won few accolades from the mature Shaw—though his childhood captivation is, as we have seen, a separate matter. In Dickens's later, darker novels—those that caused his contemporaries and two or three succeeding generations to misconstrue the progress of his art (virtually accusing him of "burnout")—and in his most innovative phase Shaw saw the most to praise. Yet, the dilemma in which Shaw sought to pit perfection against originality was not so easily settled and often returned to complicate his critical endeavors.

Just as the comparison of Dickens to Mozart was a natural association for Shaw, so he frequently drew parallels between Dickens and Shakespeare—perpetuating what had been for his generation a critical commonplace. The novelty, of course, was introduced when Shaw cast himself as the third member of the triumvirate in the *Three Plays for Puritans* preface, "Better Than Shakespear?" Not surprisingly, Shaw found both the others unsatisfactory and disappointing as "artist-philosophers," "the only sort I take quite seriously," but seemed to find them nonetheless irresistible, declaring in the preface to *Man and Superman*:

> I read Dickens and Shakespear without shame or stint; but their pregnant observations of life are not coordinated into any philosophy or religion: on the contrary, Dickens's sentimental assumptions are violently contradicted by his observations; and Shakespear's pessimism is only his wounded humanity. Both have the specific genius of the fictionist and the common sympathies of human feeling and thought in preeminent degree. They are often saner and shrewder than the philosophers just as Sancho Panza was often saner and shrewder than Don Quixote. They clear away vast masses of oppressive gravity by their sense of the ridiculous, which is at bottom a combination of sound moral judgment with lighthearted good humor. But they are concerned with the diversities of the world instead of with its unities.[50]

All of which is perhaps another way of saying that, although both Shaw and Dickens were extremely sensitive to social disorder, Shaw, the Socialist, had a cause while Dickens—and, by extension, Shakespeare—did not.

For comic Shaw, the works of Shakespeare, Dickens, Scott, and Dumas were supreme in the delightful and "very entertaining art of mimicry," through which all achieved a distinctive " 'delineation of character.' "[51] However, according to skeptic Shaw, all four lacked "an original moral standpoint," "accepting the current morality and religion ready made without any question,"[52] and consequently deserving to be consigned to the second order of literature. The affection that Shaw reserved for Dickens was, it is clear, not extended so openhandedly to Shakespeare. In the 1910 preface to *The Dark Lady of the Sonnets* on bardolatry, Shaw complained that "we know much more about Shakespear [from his works] than we know about Dickens or Thackeray."[53] Disappointment about the scant extent to which Dickens engaged in self-revelatory art would be echoed by Shaw again—and perhaps points to an unstated longing for Dickens to minister to adult concerns as powerfully as he had to the crises of childhood. Still, for dramatic caricature, Dickens came out ahead: "Dogberry is seen to be a cheap performance in comparison with the best comic figures of Cervantes, Scott, and Dickens."[54]

Brilliant specific talent spelled for Shaw at once a blessing and an insurmountable handicap. Both Dickens and Shakespeare, he noted, are forced to rely on "the common stockpot of melodramatic plots" and both have trouble motivating a "serious positive character" unless it first makes them laugh.[55] While finding both Dickens and Shakespeare skilled in rendering their characters lifelike and creating the illusion of verisimilitude, Shaw discovers the limitation that the actions of these lifelike characters are "forced on them from without." Sounding like Matthew Arnold faulting Chaucer for a want of "high seriousness" and at the same time like some of his own detractors, Shaw demonstrated that he transcended the hackneyed image that reduced Dickens to the role of the jaunty public entertainer and hearthside comforter.

A recurrent problem for Shaw was to justify his attachment to Dickens without seeming to desert the Socialist principles he imbibed in the 1880s. Although his references to Dickens's novels indicate that he knew the entire canon intimately, Shaw publicly embraced the later Dickens while acknowledging near disdain for the early, more popular works—though he drew on these heavily for metaphor as countless incidental references to Mr. Pickwick, Sam Weller, Wackford Squeers, Pecksniff, and Sairey Gamp demonstrate. Some of the most astringent comments on this subject are found in a lecture entitled "Fiction and Truth," delivered in 1887. Addressing the ironic question "whether a writer of Fiction is anything better than a mere liar," Shaw observed that in Dickens's case, "The difference between the Dickens who wrote Pickwick and the Dickens who wrote Great Expectations is analogous to the difference between a funny street boy and Schopenhauer." Shaw claimed that up to 1850 "no critic of wide and deep culture could have read Dickens without occasionally being offended and annoyed by his shortcomings";[56] 1850 was the year of *David Copperfield.*

While remaining aloof from the worshippers of Dingley Dell and the Great White Horse, Shaw distinguished his own attitude from the snobbish prejudices of the G. H. Lewes set: "I by no means pretend that all the critics who condemned Dickens are to be defended on this ground; for the more he improved the less many of them liked him." On the other hand, the "gross feasts of turkey and sausage, pudding, and brandy-and-water" that Dickens helped to institutionalize as the English Christmas held no appeal for the abstemious vegetarian G. B. S., while he viewed Little Nell as "of course nothing but a sort of literary onion, to make you cry."[57]

Shaw might well shock Dickensians by his pronouncement in the same lecture that "No equally gifted man was ever less of an artist and philosopher than he was in 1835 when, in his 23rd year, he wrote the Sketches by Boz in a fashion which Bulwer Lytton or Macaulay would have been ashamed of in their teens."[58] This casual and perhaps exaggerated dismissal of the *Sketches* runs counter to the warmer critical winds of the second half of the twentieth century that have hailed Dickens's first effort as a prelude to dazzling achievement. Of his own earliest fictional efforts, Shaw spoke with equally blunt disparagement: "They were all jéjune and rotten."[59] In the early Dickens, nevertheless, Shaw saw nothing revealed so much as defects in education, an inadequacy that Sonny Shaw had been too young to perceive, but which might have been his own autobiography as well:

> He could read and write, and had no doubt been taught a little history and geography, the simpler operations in arithmetic, a book or two of Euclid, some Latin grammar and shorthand. He had done much desultory reading and had been through works by such great writers as Shakspere, Bunyan, Swift, and Goldsmith; but he had not a student's knowledge of them, through he had his own peculiar insight to certain sides of them.

Denied the preparation and advantages of a De Quincey, a George Eliot, or—for that matter—a Shaw, Dickens made do with the tools at hand. "He had a shabby genteel knowledge of society, a Londoner's knowledge of outdoor incident, and a reporter's knowledge of public life, besides his genius, which enabled him to succeed easily in spite of the inadequacy of the rest of the equipment."[60] While Dickens was thus able to speak a language his audience understood, the deficiency was obvious to the sophisticated and gave rise to the persistent cry that Boz was " 'no gentleman,' " a cognomen Shaw employed as a pseudonym in 1889 in the *Penny Illustrated Paper*. According to Shaw, who knew too well the pangs of social ostracism, Dickens would eventually cause everyone to revise the estimate; but in unveiling the master's innocence, Shaw made clear the distance that had to be traveled:

> [A]t first he seems to have regarded all social phenomena as fortuitous and unconnected; he had neither knowledge of science nor

science of knowledge, no philosophy of history, no system of ethics, no grounding of economics, no suspicion of the theories that were behind the abuses he attacked, much less of the social conditions behind the theories; and the gentlemen who were provided with secondhand academic articles of this description despised him accordingly. Much of the abuse he got from them was richly deserved.[61]

This analysis defined for Shaw the limitations of Dickens's early criticism of society in such works as *Oliver Twist* and *Nicholas Nickleby* and justified the opinion that "His last four completed novels [*Hard Times, Little Dorrit, Great Expectations, Our Mutual Friend*] form the only part of his work which placed him above all his contemporaries as a master of fiction."[62]

Admittedly harping on the educational debility of his subject, Shaw found Dickens's principal rival, Thackeray, similarly lacking in organized knowledge. Thackeray, he noted, had been to the university "but, as he did not work there, he was fully as ignorant as Dickens when he left it." Moreover, Thackeray took away a sense of "class feeling" that Dickens fortunately escaped. The comparison served to set Dickens, like G. B. S. once a regular reader at the British Museum, in a more flattering light. "In the slang of our day," Shaw mused, "it might be said that one of these eminent novelists started as a cad; the other as a snob; and that the cad proved the better equipped of the two." Try as he might to avoid its pangs, which could not but touch him personally, Shaw phrased the embarrassing truth bluntly: "In their lack of education proper they were on equal terms. I think they were both the worse for it; and that they blundered and failed in many points to the end of their careers for want of . . . mental training."[63] The harshness of his formulation never escaped Shaw, and seven years later in a letter to Henry Arthur Jones he raised the painful, sensitive topic again:

> Have you ever considered the case of Dickens carefully? Don't you think his last (and greatest) works would have been much greater if he had had something of the systematic philosophical, historical, economic, and above all, artistic training of Goethe? I grant you it is a difficult question; but surely so fine a spirit could have been rescued from the reproach of being a Philistine, a guzzler, and an ignorantly contemptuous reporter-politician?[64]

A palpable insecurity comes through in passages like these in which

G. B. S. seems almost to plead his own case, parti pris as it were. Each fresh critical encounter with Dickens would prompt Shaw to open the wound anew.

Shaw, then, had little in common with the typical dues-paying, worshipful Dickensians, who in their undiscriminating appreciation of Dickens frequently "chose that circumstance to commend their friend by wherein he most faulted," as Ben Jonson wrote of his illustrious contemporary.[65] While Shaw made his anti-antiquarian prejudices clear in his 1889 Broadstairs Christmas piece written as Corno di Bassetto,[66] the Yuletide emergence of Squire Bancroft, the actor, from retirement seven years later for the purpose of giving readings from Dickens's *A Christmas Carol* to benefit hospitals drew a withering response. Bancroft's grand gesture, almost universally admired in the press, was to Shaw an act of pure self-indulgence "following the ordinary custom of English sportsmen of independent means."[67] Operating under the pleasing illusion that he was doing the public a service, Bancroft was in reality giving the government a chance to shirk its responsibility to maintain hospitals. According to Shaw, the officials might just as well have asked Bancroft to fix the city lights and pave the streets. Although he cheerfully risked being labeled a Scrooge, Shaw believed a progressive age that had received *A Doll's House* and Karl Marx must update its perceptions of Dickens. He resented the use (and abuse) of Dickens's name and reputation in causes that would undermine the social revolution of which the novelist himself was an unconscious herald.

Although he saw many dramatized versions of Dickens's works, Shaw seems never to have approved of a single performance.[68] Yet Shaw saw Dickens himself as a born actor who was about to go on the stage before "colossal and overwhelming literary success" caught up with him. Shaw noted that thereafter Dickens was never happy unless he was getting up some kind of acting performance. In a curious statement, which speaks to the preoccupations and manias of all artists, Shaw perceived that Dickens "finally . . . definitely became an actor in the most extreme and concentrated form—that is to say, the actor who plays all the parts in the play himself." Understanding that the novelist killed himself in his addiction to dramatic recitations, Shaw did "not expect Charles

Dickens to have any prejudice against the theatre of the ordinary kind—of the kind of the parent who imagines that the theatre is the gate of hell."[69] Nonetheless, Shaw recorded his wonder that Dickens, in the real life role of Victorian father, absolutely refused to let his daughter entertain ideas of a theatrical career.

Histrionic wiles aside, it was really Dickens the energetic social critic to whom Shaw most hearkened. It was the Dickens of sufficient breadth of creative vision to encompass a nation and an age that Shaw applauded as he wrote, "Dickens's England, the England of Barnacle and Stiltstalking and Hamlet's Aunt, invaded and overwhelmed by Merdle and Veneering and Fledgeby, with Mr. Gradgrind theorising, and Mr. Bounderby bullying in the provinces, is revealing itself in every day's news, as the real England we live in."[70] In thus taking the sum of the subject's parts, Shaw described a Dickens who might not have been recognizable in the Victorian setting, or particularly welcomed among his worshippers in the succeeding generation. However, this is the Dickens—if somewhat leaner and rangier from subsistence on Fabian "vegetable love"—who has become increasingly familiar, sympathetic, and understandable ever since. With even the slightest consciousness of his own appetite for paradox, G. B. S. could scarcely be surprised that as he held the glass up to Dickens what he most admired were, inevitably, reflections of Shaw.

iii

While Shaw advertised his aversion to all manner of Dickensian stage business in the hands of others, as evidenced in his reviews of theatrical versions of the novelist's works, he showed no such reluctance when it came to making use of Dickens's creations in his own plays. Indeed, as we have seen, he often went out of his way to point out characters and scenes borrowed or pillaged; "all is fish that comes to my net," he wrote.[71] He once estimated that if someone were to count the allusions in his literary works, those to Dickens would outnumber all those to any other writer by a ratio of four to one.[72] The fertile world of Dickens's novels served Shaw as a vast garden from which to pluck the ready allusion, the illustrative witticism, and the characteristic metaphor for his prefaces and essays as well as for his voluminous correspondence. His full awareness of the influence suggests that this involvement became not only profound, but highly personal, and to a rare degree a conscious device and a rhetorical tool.

Shaw's creative work is filled with Dickensian emanations and resonances; it will serve our purpose here merely to highlight several indisputable examples. Part of the trick of producing "an effect of daring innovation and originality," Shaw confessed when recalling his days of novel-writing was "to lift characters bodily out of the pages of Charles Dickens."[73] Thus, it is hardly surprising to find in *Widowers' Houses* (1892) two characters, Sartorius and Lickcheese, whom St. John Ervine was first to recognize as "derived, not only in nature and relationship, but in actual situation, from Casby, the owner of Bleeding Heart Yard in *Little Dorrit,* and Pancks, his rent collector."[74] In his determined effort to shock respectable society with *Plays Unpleasant*—and with consciousness of his own dreary background as a collector of rents in Dublin—Shaw selected the most appalling aspect of Dickens's strangely subversive novel around which to build his first play.

The biting, satirical tone of *Widowers' Houses* transmits as well the savagery of Dickens's indictment of industrial society, *Hard Times.* Casby is scarcely different in outlook from Josiah Bounderby of Coketown while Sartorius is a less genial version of John Tarleton, the underwear manufacturer of *Misalliance.* Shaw's socialist interest in the origins of capital and its effect on those who possess it is a recurrent theme in his writings—culminating dramatically in *Major Barbara* (1905) and in expository form in *The Intelligent Woman's Guide to Socialism and Capitalism* (1928).

Shaw's artistic debt to Dickens is further recalled in *Widowers' Houses* when Dr. Harry Trench is faced with the unwelcome recognition that his own private income is derived from the interest on the rent of slum hovels, a scene reminiscent of the pivotal moment of Aristotelian irony of *Great Expectations* in which the convict Magwitch confronts Pip with the source of the latter's fortune and the means that have transformed a blacksmith's boy into a gentleman.[75] For both heroes the confrontation and the crisis of disillusionment are starting points for moral regeneration, or as Ellie Dunn later expressed it in *Heartbreak House,* "the end of happiness and the beginning of peace."

Yet there are differences, as one would expect, between the

Shavian and Dickensian approach. In Dickens, villains and land-lords are generally monsters and grotesques, and when they are not susceptible—like Ebenezer Scrooge—to miraculous conversion, veritable gargoyles. Shaw's characters in *Widowers' Houses* and elsewhere are mainly civilized, completely believable, occasionally despicable human beings. But that, after all, is Shaw's message. Moreover, Shaw's fidelity to Ibsen-like realism accounts for the special punch of this "Unpleasant" play. In an important thematic respect, however, Shaw's perception of the rotten base of capitalist society founded on industrialism and exploitation parallels Dickens's own vision in his major works.

The character of Bohun, Q.C., in *You Never Can Tell* (1895–97), once Shaw's most popular play, is a direct projection of the Old Bailey lawyer Jaggers in *Great Expectations*. Shaw freely acknowledged the debt in 1898.[76] Jaggers, complete with nervous habits of biting the side of his forefinger, throwing his hulking frame into ungainly postures, and compulsively washing his hands following interviews with clients, is an unusually vital and ambiguous character—even for Dickens. When Shaw created his first lawyer in the drama, the powerful image of Jaggers intruded itself upon his imagination. Hefty, clean-shaven, with black hair, bristling eyebrows, sharp manner, and above all the stentorian voice, Jaggers and Bohun are one. The principal difference, in complexion, is one of exact contrast. Like Jaggers, whose humane instincts are revealed when he intervenes to rescue Estella, the child of the deported Magwitch and the savage tramp Molly, Bohun mellows after pronouncing his judgment and emits a softer glow.

In his notes to *Caesar and Cleopatra* (1898) Shaw identified Britannus, Caesar's slave and a conscious satire on the stereotype Briton, as an early version of Dicken's obstinate and complacent, quintessentially English businessman, Mr. Podsnap of *Our Mutual Friend*:

> But Britannus . . . represents the unadulterated Briton who fought Caesar and impressed Roman observers much as we should expect the ancestors of Mr Podsnap to impress the cultivated Italians of their time.[77]

Even against the learned objections of classicist Gilbert Murray, G.B.S. defended his Dickensian portrait:

> I also demur to your dictum that we have enough information about
> the ancient Britons to shew that they were not like [Britannus]. In
> every line that I have come across concerning them I see Mr
> Podsnap.[78]

Suspicious and at once fearful, Shaw's Britannus holds himself
aloof from frivolous Italians and machines "not of British
design,"[79] while Dickens's Podsnap talks to foreigners as if they
were children hard of hearing and is astonished by the "discovery
he has made that Italy is not England."[80]

Victorian prudery is yet another trait shared by Britannus and
Podsnap. Shaw's ancient Briton is scandalized by the marital
arrangements of the Egyptian royalty and professes shock by
Cleopatra's presence before Caesar without a chaperone. Likewise,
Mr. Podsnap's attentions to his daughter, "a certain institution . . . called 'the young person,'" are governed by one overriding
principle: "The question about everything was, would it bring a
blush into the cheek of the young person?"[81] As a result, Georgiana
is restricted to companionship with older persons and heavy, pon-
derous furniture and is solemnly forbidden conversation that
touches on "bodies in rivers" or starvation in the London streets.
Oppressed with vague notions of honor and anxious lest Caesar
"be seen in the fashionable part of Alexandria" before changing his
wet toga, Britannus expresses the essence of Podsnappery in urging
the Roman "to regard life seriously, as men do in my country!"[82] It
can scarcely be doubted that Dickens and Shaw were in these
instances drawing beads on the same lumbering target.

Perhaps Shaw's most Dickensian play, *Major Barbara* (1905) is
like nothing so much as Dickens's exploration of Coketown
revisited, revised—and very nearly inverted. Or, as Shaw reminds
us in the preface, he is set to attack the Christian social myth
propounded by "Dickens' doctor in the debtor's prison [*Little
Dorrit*], who tells the newcomer of its ineffable peace and security:
no duns; no tyrannical collectors of rates, taxes, and rent; no
importunate hopes nor exacting duties; nothing but the rest and
safety of having no farther to fall."[83] Shaw's accurate revival of
Doctor Haggage's sentiments illustrates the conviction that both
the debtor's prison and the Salvation Army confine humanity at the
same dismal level, the latter—in Andrew Undershaft's words—

administering "bread and treacle and dreams of heaven." Snobby Price seems almost to echo Haggage's ideal: "I've got the piece that I value more; and thats the peace that passeth hall hannerstennin."[84]

Moreover, Barbara's well-intended ministrations to the London poor recall a similar episode in *Bleak House*, in which Esther Summerson and Ada Clare confront working-class squalor in their visit to the brickmaker's family, sullen, diseased, dissipated, and brutalized, in their hovel. While, however, the recipients of charity in Act II of *Major Barbara* may be cynical about their reduced circumstances, Shaw makes a deliberate effort to capture in Bill Walker not only the loutish degeneracy but also the sullen, embittered outrage of Dickens's brickmaker, who responds frankly to the harping of the do-gooder Mrs. Pardiggle:

> I wants a end of these liberties took with my place. I wants a end of being drawed like a badger. Now you're a-going to poll-pry and question according to custom—I know what you're a-going to be up to. . . . Is my daughter a-washin? Yes, she *is* a washin. Look at the water. Smell it! That's wot we drinks. How do you like it, and what do you think of gin instead! An't my place dirty? Yes, it is dirty—it's nat'rally dirty, and it's nat'rally onwholesome; and we've had five dirty and onwholesome children, as is all dead infants, and so much the better for them, and for us besides. Have I read the little book wot you left? No, I an't read the little book wot you left. There an't nobody here as knows how to read it; and if there wos, it wouldn't be suitable to me. It's a book fit for a babby, and I'm not a babby. . . . How have I been conducting of myself? Why, I've been drunk for three days; and I'da been drunk four if I'da had the money. Don't I never mean for to go to church? No, I don't never mean for to go to church. I shouldn't be expected there, if I did. . . . And how did my wife get that black eye? Why, I give it her; and if she says I didn't, she's a lie![85]

Bill Walker, while more laconic, is one with Dickens's brickmaker in shocking sensibilities by his confessed brutality and the threat of more. Indeed, the brickmaker's catalog of grievances is, in rhetorical structure and tone, parallel to Shaw's exegesis in the preface to *Major Barbara*:

> Now what does this Let Him Be Poor mean? It means let him be weak. Let him be ignorant. Let him become a nucleus of disease. Let him be a standing exhibition and example of ugliness and dirt. Let

him have rickety children. . . . Let his habitations turn our cities into poisonous congeries of slums. Let his daughters infect our young men with the diseases of the streets, and his sons revenge him by turning the nation's manhood into scrofula, cowardice, cruelty, hypocrisy, political imbecility, and all the other fruits of oppression and malnutrition. Let the undeserving become still less deserving; and let the deserving lay up for himself, not treasures in heaven, but horrors in hell upon earth.[86]

Just as the bubbly, enthusiastic Salvation Army Commissioner Mrs. Baines is a rough paraphrase of Mrs. Pardiggle's earnest officiousness, so Bill Walker's unwavering refusal to swallow the Army's doctrines or to yield to its liberal hypocrisies echoes the poignant but inarticulate needling of Dickens's brickmaker. While Mrs. Baines solicits contributions from a whiskey distiller and a munitions manufacturer, Bill Walker's taunting refrain "Wot prawce selvytion nah?" evokes the attitude of the brickmaker and at the same time parallels the epiphany Barbara herself is approaching. The association with *Bleak House* gains strength when we reflect that Barbara sees through the contradiction between Mrs. Baines's doctrine and her ultimate dependence on "tainted" money in just the same way that Esther Summerson is alert to Mrs. Pardiggle's "too businesslike and systematic" manner of dispensing her wisdom as well as the grotesque incongruity of the matron's own "unnaturally constrained children" forced to subscribe their shillings and pence to charitable causes. One difference in the philosophies of *Bleak House* and *Major Barbara* is that Dickens, knowing all their problems, had no clear sense of what to do about the poor; Ada sheds tears over Jenny's dead infant while Esther dresses the brickmaker's family in mystery and sentiment: "I think the best side of such people is almost hidden from us. What the poor are to the poor is little known, excepting to themselves and God."[87] Shaw couldn't digest this concoction of faith and illusion, and offers Andrew Undershaft and Act III as an antidote.

As much as Undershaft seems an inversion of Dickens's oppressive capitalist Bounderby, Shaw's ironically approving portrait bears an even more commanding resemblance to a lesser known, minor character in *Bleak House*, the ingenious son of the Dedlocks' housekeeper and older brother of Trooper George, the millionaire ironmaster and upstart activist in the parliamentary elections, formidable Mr. Rouncewell. In fact, the sympathetically drawn Rouncewell is a prototype of the odious Bounderby in *Hard Times,* which appeared in 1854, the year after *Bleak House* was finished. In addition to being "self-made," both tycoons are estranged from their mothers and have consciously cut themselves off from a former way of life. Rouncewell's dukedom of the northern iron country, in which "coal pits and ashes, high chimneys and red bricks, blighted verdure, scorching fires, and a heavy, never-lightening cloud of smoke become the features of the scenery," complete with a "black canal bridge" and the "clang of iron," seems an obvious inspiration for Coketown in *Hard Times.* However, unlike Bounderby's world of wrenching toil and endless, heart-breaking drudgery, Rouncewell's orderly factories are places of prodigious and honest industry—where poor men find opportunity and dignity as they do at Perivale St. Andrews. What appeals to Dickens in *Bleak House* is the positive, creative aspect of the new industry, an attitude comparable to Shaw's perspective on the armaments factory in *Major Barbara.* Trooper George pauses in wonder at the gateway of Rouncewell's as he beholds "a great perplexity of iron lying about in every stage and in a vast variety of shapes—in bars, in wedges, in sheets; in tanks, in boilers, in axles, in wheels, in cogs, in cranks, in rails; twisted and wrenched into eccentric and perverse forms as separate parts of machinery."[88] Similarly, the family visitors to Undershaft's arsenal marvel at the bewildering display of technical apparatus and organization about them: the parapets, the chimney shafts, the cannon, the experimental gun carriage, the practice dummies, the firestep, the trolley, and the bombshell. From Cusins's humanist perspective, the prospect offers "Not a ray of hope. Everything perfect! wonderful! real!"[89]

Major Barbara represents a crucial stage in Shaw's creative involvement with Dickens. Barbara Undershaft takes her cue from Dickens's heroes Pip and Clennam (the latter of whom Shaw always saw as the real Dickens) and opts for the world of reality against the escape "into a paradise of enthusiasm and prayer and soul saving."[90] The moral—and *Major Barbara* is a play with a decisive moral—is stronger than anything in Dickens, tougher even, for being more comprehensive in its criticism of society, than are *Widowers' Houses* and *Mrs Warren's Profession.* Early in the third act, Barbara seems to reject the popular sentiments that cling to Dickens's public reputation as she enjoins Cusins that "There are larger loves and diviner dreams than the fireside ones"; that dream is finally the dream that is no dream. In *Major Barbara* Shaw manages to gather the loose ends that he saw dangling from Dickens's major novels, and in this act of seizure he worked out his richest Dickensian vein.

But Dickens intrudes upon the later plays as well. In *Misalliance* (1910) Shaw extracts a passage from a 1906 letter to Chesterton[91] complaining of Dickens's reserve in letters to his family and plants it, with modest retouching, in the mouth of John Tarleton:

> TARLETON. Yes, shyness. Read Dickens.
> LORD SUMMERHAYS [*surprised*] Dickens!! Of all authors, Charles Dickens! Are you serious?
> TARLETON. I dont mean his books. Read his letters to his family. Read any man's letters to his children. Theyre not human. Theyre not about himself or themselves. Theyre about hotels, scenery, about the weather, about getting wet and losing the train and what he saw on the road and all that. Not a word about himself. Forced. Shy. Duty letters. All fit to be published: that says everything.[92]

Moreover, it is clear that the opening scene of *Pygmalion* very nearly parallels the central incident of Chapter Two of the *Pickwick Papers*, in which a riot is nearly provoked by a cabman incensed at Mr. Pickwick's innocent jottings in his notebook. Eventually, Mr. Pickwick is delivered by the entry on the scene of a tall, confident stranger. Similarly, Professor Henry Higgins, oblivious to the people waiting for cabs on a rainy night at Covent Garden, is absorbed in gathering scientific information on Cockney dialect. Taken for a "tec" or "copper's nark" Higgins is beset by an indignant crowd who only lose interest when fellow linguist Colonel Pickering intervenes.

Both scenes serve to introduce the main character in a situation revealing a fundamental weakness from which springs much of the comedy generated by the same character in later action. Although their personalities are quite nearly opposite, Higgins is no more successful than Pickwick in representing his intentions to London passersby. Even the social comment in the two scenes originates in a similar distrust of the upper, or educated, classes by the lower ranks. Nearly one hundred years separate the events of Shaw's play and the adventures of Mr. Pickwick, but class hostility was evidently as sensitive and explosive in the reign of George V as in pre-Victorian London.

In the same play dustman Alfred Doolittle's sudden good fortune recalls that of Dickens's Golden Dustman, Noddy Boffin, in *Our Mutual Friend,* while the waterman's daughter Lizzie Hexam in the same novel is taken up by the gentleman Eugene Wrayburn in a fashion not unlike flower girl Eliza Doolittle's elevation in *Pygmalion.* The possibilities, thus, of isolating Dickensian presences in Shaw's plays seem limitless.

At the same time Dickens was a medium for communicating with a public that probably knew its once favorite novelist somewhat better than its Testament and undoubtedly better than Marx or Ibsen—for whom, to some extent, Dickens was a more publicly palatable surrogate. A typical instance in which Shaw wraps Dickens into a topical reference appears in one of his last letters to *The Times* as, in his nineties, he weighed the perennial question of capital punishment:

> The police are not impartial. They must do everything in their power to obtain a conviction. As one of Dickens's characters put it, "Much better hang the wrong fellow than no fellow."[93]

The Dickens character sponsoring this policy is no less than the baronet's cousin in *Bleak House,* reacting to the failure of the detectives to apprehend the murderer of Sir Leicester Dedlock's solicitor, Tulkinghorn. Getting good mileage from the Dickensian recollections, Shaw in 1947 was only polishing up the same allusion he used thirty-one years earlier, in the preface to *Androcles and the Lion,* when expressing his idea of primitive justice as "partly legalized revenge and partly expiation by sacrifice."[94]

Shaw was conscious of Dickens's analysis of the class struggle as he recalled an event from his childhood in which his father was shocked to find Sonny playing with a son of an ironmonger who—while financially better fixed than Shaw Senior, an unsuccessful wholesaler of flour—was of a lower caste. Shaw speculated that "Even when intermarriage does take place, you have the result described by Dickens in Dombey and Son, where Mrs Dombey's set could not be induced to mix with Mr Dombey's set, and the two occupied different ends of the drawingroom."[95] In another instance, he presumed that everyone remembered "the middle class gentleman in Dickens's novel who was so disgusted because a government clerk told him to shut the door after him, as he was letting in a devil of a draught."[96] On redistribution of income, Shaw dealt with the prospect that monopolies would destroy "the personal independence of the middle class, and [turn] Mr Pickwick into Mr Wilfer."[97]

In answer to Nazi anti-Semitic ethnology, and by-the-way disarming criticism that *The Adventures of the Black Girl in Her Search for God* smiled on racial prejudice, Shaw declared that "this Chosen Race business is not Socialism, but, as my late colleague Charles Dickens expressed it, 'So far from it, on the contrary, quite the reverse.'"[98] Shaw brought his intricate knowledge of Dickens to bear on nearly every enthusiasm or cause that he happened to pursue. From Dickens's attack on brutal schoolmasters in *Nicholas Nickleby*, Shaw drew Mrs. Wackford Squeers and Dotheboys Hall into the antivaccination controversy. Holding out for an enlightenment in bacteriological therapeutics, Shaw observed in a 1906 letter to Charles Gane, the Secretary of the National Anti-Vaccination League, that "Mrs. Squeers's method of opening abscesses with an inky penknife is far less repugnant to modern surgeons than the Local Government Board's method of inoculating children with casual dirt moistened with an undefined pathogenic substance obtained from calves is to modern bacteriologists."[99] Lecturing in 1889 on the dissolution of the German National Assembly by King Frederick William IV, Shaw observed that the President of the Assembly was carried out in his chair and deposited by the soldiers in the street "much as Captain Boldwig removed Mr Pickwick to the pound."[100]

A bleak outlook on the possibility for meaningful change in the processes of government and society, Shaw reminds us, he shares with Dickens: "Everything is to be changed and nothing is to be changed. . . . And the word of Dickens is to be justified."[101] Dickens finally came to perceive, Shaw felt, that government and the institutions of society were corrupt throughout. This perception became the turning point of his career, marking the entrance of the novelist as social prophet and the transformation of Pickwick into Merdle. Dismayed at the normal human tendency to evade reality and welcome fantasy, Shaw invoked "Mr. Podsnap [who] always swept disagreeable considerations behind him and refused to discuss them, or to associate with people who did discuss them."[102]

As a modern interpreter of Socialism and Capitalism, Shaw felt some need to explain his delight in the nineteenth-century writers, doubting whether Dickens in particular could be as "entertaining" to a contemporary audience as "to me, who spent the first forty-four years of my life in that benighted period."[103] Elsewhere: "[N]ineteenth century poets and prophets who denounced the wickedness of our Capitalism . . . are much more exciting to read than the economists and writers on political science who worked out the economic theory and political requirements of Socialism. Carlyle's Past and Present and Shooting Niagara, Ruskin's Ethics of the Dust and Fors Clavigera, William Morris's News from Nowhere . . . , Dickens's Hard Times and Little Dorrit, are notable examples."[104] Emphasizing the essentially middle-class origins of the Socialist revolt, he defied "any navvy, or any duke, to maul the middle class as Dickens mauled it."[105]

The full range of human experience seems at times to pass through Shaw's Dickensian prism. The brilliance of Dickensian caricatures—especially of the minor characters—is always at the forefront of Shaw's mind.[106] Moreover, while most of Shaw's drama is focused on upper-middle-class problems and mores, the vast gallery of lower class or shabby-genteel characters in his plays—as earlier in his novels—are basically Dickensian in inspiration. Sartorius and Lickcheese (*Widowers' Houses*), Kitty Warren (*Mrs Warren's Profession*), Burgess (*Candida*), the Waiter (*You Never Can Tell*), Drinkwater (*Captain Brassbound's Conversion*), Henry Straker (*Man and Superman*), Haffigan (*John Bull's Other Island*), Snobby Price, Rummy Mitchens, Peter Shirley, and Bill Walker (*Major Barbara*), Mrs. George (*Getting Married*), "Gunner" (*Misalliance*), Nurse Guinness and Billy Dunn (*Heartbreak House*), the English soldier (*Saint Joan*), "Sweetie" (*Too True To Be Good*), and, of course, Alfred Doolittle (*Pygmalion*): all of these owe something and several nearly everything to Dickens's models.

The Dickens metaphor suffused Shaw's everyday language to an extent that obfuscation is sometimes a real danger. Yet, all his life Shaw tapped his nineteenth-century hero for the apt phrase, the bright illustration, not so much to clarify as to color and embellish his pronouncement on the issue at hand. As the twentieth century wore on, it was only natural for him, as a child of the nineteenth, to become more conscious of the disparity between his mid-Victorian origins and the world that presented itself to him at middle age. His references to Dickens, steady in volume throughout his career, became not only a way of paying tribute to the novelist's genius and of shoring up a waning critical reputation—before the Rediscovery heralded by Wilson and Orwell—but also served as an atonement for the book G.B.S. never found time to write.

Dan H. Laurence

Martin Quinn

Notes

[1] "24 May 1893," in Shaw, *Music in London 1890–94* (London: Constable, 1932), II, 316.

[2] Archibald Henderson, *George Bernard Shaw: Man of the Century* (New York: Appleton-Century-Crofts, 1956), p. 31.

[3] "24 May 1893," *Music in London*, II, 315.

[4] W. Walter Crotch, "The Decline—And After!" *The Dickensian*, 15 (July 1919), 124.

[5] *The Dickensian*, 15 (July 1919), 124.

[6] "Charles Dickens: Some Personal Recollections and Opinions," *The Bookman*, 41 (February 1912), 247.

[7] Edgar Johnson, *Charles Dickens: His Tragedy and Triumph* (New York: Simon and Schuster, 1952), II, 938, 1068.

[8] Blanche Patch, *Thirty Years with G.B.S.* (New York: Dodd, Mead, 1951), p. 190.

[9] Mrs. Georgina Gillmore Musters, Shaw's half first cousin (the daughter of Shaw's mother's half-sister) recollected in a letter that her aunt, G.B.S.'s mother, was herself a voracious reader of fiction and especially the novels of Dickens. Like her famous son, she apparently knew the Dickens characters "as though they belonged to her circle of friends." See Henderson, *George Bernard Shaw: Man of the Century*, pp. 87–88.

[10] Johnson, *Charles Dickens: His Tragedy and Triumph*, I, 34, 45.

[11] "Shame and Wounded Snobbery: A Secret Kept for 80 Years," in Shaw, *Sixteen Self Sketches* (New York: Dodd, Mead, 1949), p. 43.

[12] B.C. Rosset, *Shaw of Dublin: The Formative Years* (University Park, Pennsylvania: Pennsylvania State University Press, 1964), pp. 135–174.

[13] Shaw, *Collected Letters: 1898–1910*, ed. Dan H. Laurence (New York: Dodd, Mead, 1972), p. 652 (14 September 1906).

[14] Shaw, *Collected Plays with their Prefaces* (New York: Dodd, Mead, 1975), IV, 32.

[15] Letter to Gilbert Murray, 14 March 1911, in Shaw, *Collected Letters 1911–1925;* ed. Dan H. Laurence (New York: Viking Press, 1985), pp. 17–18.

[16] Shaw, *Collected Letters: 1874–1897*, ed. Dan H. Laurence (New York: Dodd, Mead, 1965), p. 773 (11 June 1897).

[17] Letter to Esmé Percy, 22 September 1941 (Humanities Research Center, University of Texas at Austin).

[18] John Forster, *The Life of Charles Dickens* (London: J.M. Dent, 1927), I, 32.

[19] *Collected Plays with Their Prefaces*, II, 33 (Preface to *The Devil's Disciple*).

[20] Hesketh Pearson, *Bernard Shaw: His Life and Personality* (London: Collins, 1942), p. 200.

[21] Charles MacMahon Shaw, *Bernard's Brethren* (London: Constable, 1939), pp. 125–26.

[22]Shaw was of the firm belief that children ought not to be exploited on the stage. Thus, while the Morells and the Hushabyes speak of children, they are not visible. The only youngsters who actually make an appearance in Shaw's plays are those for whom there is historical and dramaturgical necessity, such as the boy king Ptolemy in *Caesar and Cleopatra*, the seven-year-old John of Gaunt in *The Six of Calais*, and Dunois' page in *Saint Joan*.

[23]See letters to William Archer, *Collected Letters: 1874–1897*, pp. 400–01 (21 August 1893), and *Collected Letters: 1898–1910*, p. 359 (2 September 1903).

[24]Hugh Kingsmill, "Shaw and Dickens," *The Progress of a Biographer* (London: Methuen, 1949), p. 51.

[25]Johnson, *II, 651*.

[26]*Sixteen Self Sketches*, p. 151.

[27]"Redistribution of Income," in Shaw, *The Road to Equality: Ten Unpublished Lectures and Essays*, ed. Louis Crompton (Boston: Beacon Press, 1971), p. 242.

[28]Henderson, p. 166.

[29]Johnson, II, 798, 930–35, 1006.

[30]Johnson, II, 721. Shaw conveyed this information to Edgar Johnson in the summer of 1946. See Johnson's acknowledgment, part 7, chapter 8, note 11.

[31]"'This Ever-Diverse Pair,'" *Time and Tide*, 27 July 1935, pp. 1111–12.

[32]For records of Mrs. Perugini's genre paintings, many exhibited at the Royal Academy, and for the work of her second husband, Charles (Carlo) Edward Perugini (1839–1918), born in Italy, see *Cyclopedia of Painters and Paintings*, ed. J.D. Champlin (1913), volume 3, and *Allgemeines Lexikon der bildenden Kunstter von der Antike bis zur Gegenwart . . .*, eds. J. Thieme and F. Becher (1907–50), volume 26.
Neither husband nor wife shrank from illustrations of Dickens's more sentimental themes.

[33]Gladys Storey, *Dickens and Daughter* (London: Frederick Muller, 1939), pp. 173–74.

[34]*Mr. and Mrs. Charles Dickens: His Letters to Her*, ed. Walter Dexter (London: Constable, 1935), xi. Although Mrs. Perugini said that her mother gave the letters directly to her, Dexter claimed that they were passed to Kate on the death of her sister Mamie in 1896. (See "Editor's Introductory Note, " x.)

[35]Johnson, I, 431; II, 751.

[36]Mrs. Perugini opened her soul to Shaw on 9 December 1897 in a letter that she asked him to burn. For Shaw's note to this effect, inserted in the black-bordered mourning envelope, see Section II of this book, p. 62.

[37]*Time and Tide*, 27 July 1935, p. 1111.

[38]*Mr. and Mrs. Charles Dickens*, x–xi.

[39]*Collected Letters: 1898–1910*, p. 762 (1 March 1908).

[40]Thomas Wright, *The Life of Charles Dickens* (London: Herbert Jenkins, 1935).

[41]See note 33.

[42]"Dickens and Mrs. Perugini," *Times Literary Supplement*, 29 July 1939, p. 453.

[43]Preface to *Great Expectations* (New York: Limited Editions Club, 1937), xix.

[44]*Collected Letters: 1898–1910*, p. 927 (5 June 1910).

[45]"Mr. J.B. Priestley on the Immortal Memory of Dickens," *The Dickensian*, 28 (Spring 1932), 139.

[46]Edmund Wilson, "Dickens: The Two Scrooges," *The Wound and the Bow* (1947; rpt. New York: Oxford University Press, 1965), pp. 4–5.

[47]George H. Ford, *Dickens and His Readers: Aspects of Novel-Criticism Since 1836* (1955; rpt. New York: W.W. Norton, 1965), pp. 233, 242.

[48]"9 December 1891," *Music in London*, I, 294. Thomas Mayne Reid was an Irish novelist who specialized in romances and adventure stories beloved by young boys.

[49]"Mr. Heinemann and the Censor," in Shaw, *Our Theatres in the Nineties* (London: Constable, 1932), III, 346 (2 April 1898).

[50]*Collected Plays with Their Prefaces*, II, 520.

[51]Shaw, *The Complete Prefaces* (London: Paul Hamlyn, 1965), p. 543 (*Back to Methuselah*).

[52]*Collected Letters: 1898–1910*, p. 551 (c. August 1905).

[53]*Collected Plays with Their Prefaces*, IV, 292 (*The Dark Lady of the Sonnets*).

[54]*Shaw on Theatre*, ed. E.J. West (New York: Hill and Wang, 1958), p. 102 (*Saturday Review*, 99, 11 February 1905).

[55]*Complete Plays with Their Prefaces*, II, 520–21 (*Man and Superman*).

[56]"Fiction and Truth," *Bernard Shaw's Nondramatic Literary Criticism*, ed. Stanley Weintraub (Lincoln: University of Nebraska Press, 1972), pp. 3, 12–13.

[57]"Fiction and Truth," p. 13.

[58]"Fiction and Truth," p. 12.

[59]Letter to Frederick H. Evans, 27 August 1895, in *Collected Letters 1874–1897*, p. 550.

[60]"Fiction and Truth," pp. 12–13.

[61]Ibid.

[62]"Fiction and Truth," p. 13.

[63]"Fiction and Truth," pp. 13–14.

[64]*Collected Letters: 1874–1897*, pp. 463–64 (2 December 1894).

[65]Ben Jonson, "Timber," in *Seventeenth-Century Prose and Poetry*, ed. Robert P. Tristram Coffin and Alexander M. Witherspoon (New York: Harcourt, Brace, 1957), p. 126.

[66]"Musical Mems," *The Star*, 27 December 1889; rpt. in *Shaw's Music*, ed. Dan H. Laurence (London: Bodley Head, 1981), I, pp. 879–84 (as "Christmas in Broadstairs").

[67]*Our Theatres in the Nineties*, II, 278–81.

[68]In a triple-barreled 1896 review, "Resurrection Pie," Shaw discussed *Jo*, the revival of a dramatization of *Bleak House*, which "at some remote date . . . between the drying of the Flood and the advent of Ibsen . . . shared the fate of most

of Dickens's novels in being 'adapted to the stage'" *(Our Theatres in the Nineties,* II, 134). His impression that the process of adaptation had "atrociously degraded" Dickens's masterpieces, or sub-masterpieces, is unmistakable. Shaw regretted that it had been his "fate at one time or another to witness performances founded on *Pickwick, Oliver Twist, Dombey and Son,* and *David Copperield."* Of Mrs. Oscar Beringer's *Holly Tree Inn,* an 1896 adaptation of Dickens's *Household Words* story "The Holly Tree," memorable for the appearance of Cobbs the boots, Shaw was disdainful: "It is very prettily done, and just the sort of piece that old people like" *(Our Theatres in the Nineties,* III, 8). Similarly, Shaw brushed off Ian Robertson's suggestion that he rewrite the third act of *The Devil's Disciple* (in which he had already borrowed Sydney Carton's predicament) to agree more with the romantic spirit of Freeman Wills's adaptation of *A Tale of Two Cities,* a work quaintly titled *The Only Way.* "I refuse to pander to these Renaissance sensualities," he wrote to William Archer on 24 January 1900 *(Collected Letters: 1898–1910,* p. 138). Eight years later, recalling the great success of *The Only Way,* Shaw remarked that he was "getting too old now for melodrama" *(Collected Letters: 1898–1910,* p. 751).

[69]*Shaw on Theatre,* pp. 187–188.

[70]"On Dickens," *The Dickensian,* 10 (June 1914), 151.

[71]*Collected Plays with Their Prefaces,* IV, 799 ("Mr. Shaw's 'Literary Morals,'" *The Observer,* 11 January 1914).

[72]Ford, *Dickens and His Readers,* p. 233; *Letters of Alexander Woollcott,* ed. Beatrice Kaufman and Joseph Hennessey (New York: Viking Press, 1944), p. 109 (15 March 1932). Edgar Rosenberg has collected Shaw's allusions to Dickens in published writings and correspondence, tabulating 538 individual references, as catalogued in "The Shaw/Dickens File," *The Shaw Review,* September 1977 and January 1978, and *Shaw: The Annual of Bernard Shaw Studies,* 1982. This number would, however, have been larger if Professor Rosenberg had been able to examine all of the more than four thousand entries of serial contributions in Dan H. Laurence's *Bernard Shaw: A Bibliography* (1983) and more than thirty thousand extant unpublished letters.

[73]*Collected Plays with Their Prefaces,* V, 258 *(Back to Methuselah).*

[74]St. John Ervine, *Bernard Shaw: His Life, Work, and Friends* (New York: William Morrow, 1956), pp. 245–46.

[75]Shaw would duplicate this scene in *Mrs Warren's Profession* (1893).

[76]*Collected Letters: 1898–1910,* p. 34 (21 April 1898); see also Shaw's letter to H. C. Duffin, 5 January 1920 (Arents Collection, New York Public Library).

[77]*Collected Plays with Their Prefaces,* II, 300 (Notes to *Caesar and Cleopatra).*

[78]*Collected Letters: 1898–1910,* p. 180 (28 July 1900).

[79]*Collected Plays with Their Prefaces,* II, 239 *(Caesar and Cleopatra).*

[80]Charles Dickens, *Our Mutual Friend* (rpt. New York: New American Library, 1964), xx, 278.

[81]*Our Mutual Friend,* xi, 152–53.

[82]*Collected Plays with Their Prefaces,* II, 241 *(Caesar and Cleopatra).*

[83]*Collected Plays with Their Prefaces*, III, 38–39 (Preface to *Major Barbara*).

[84]*Collected Plays with Their Prefaces*, III, 100 (*Major Barbara*).

[85]Charles Dickens, *Bleak House* (rpt. New York: New American Library, 1964), viii, 122.

[86]*Collected Plays with Their Prefaces*, III, 25 (Preface to *Major Barbara*).

[87]*Bleak House*, viii, 120–21, 124.

[88]*Bleak House*, lxiii, 848.

[89]*Collected Plays with Their Prefaces*, III, 158 (*Major Barbara*).

[90]*Collected Plays with Their Prefaces*, III, 182 (*Major Barbara*).

[91]The relevant passage of the 6 September 1906 letter to G. K. Chesterton:
> There is a curious contrast between Dickens's sentimental indiscretions concerning his marriage and his sorrows and quarrels, and his impenetrable reserve about himself as displayed in his published correspondence. He writes to his family about waiters, about hotels, about screeching tumblers of hot brandy and water, and about the seasick man in the next berth, but never one really intimate word, never a real confession of his soul. (*Collected Letters: 1898–1910*, pp. 646–47).

See also section 2 of the present book, pp. 65–67.

[92]*Collected Plays with Their Prefaces*, IV, 186–87 (*Misalliance*).

[93]"Capital Punishment," *The Times*, 5 December 1947; see Allan Chappelow, *Shaw: 'The Chucker-Out'* (London: George Allen and Unwin, 1969), p. 19.

[94]*Collected Plays with Their Prefaces*, IV, 469–70 ("Preface on the Prospects of Christianity," *Androcles and the Lion*).

[95]"The Simple Truth about Socialism," in *The Road to Equality*, pp. 187–88.

[96]"Bureaucracy and Jobbery," in *The Road to Equality*, p. 112. The reference is to Arthur Clennam in *Little Dorrit* (Book I, chapter X).

[97]"Redistribution of Income," in *The Road to Equality*, p. 268.

[98]*Shaw: 'The Chucker-Out'*, p. 201.

[99]*Collected Letters: 1898–1910*, p. 606 (22 February 1906).

[100]"The New Politics: From Lassalle to the Fabians," in *The Road to Equality*, p. 58.

[101]*Collected Plays with Their Prefaces*, III, 678 (*The Shewing-up of Blanco Posnet*).

[102]"Redistribution of Income," in *The Road to Equality*, p. 206.

[103]Appendix, *The Intelligent Woman's Guide to Socialism and Capitalism* (New York: Brentano's, 1928), p. 469.

[104]*Bernard Shaw's Nondramatic Literary Criticism*, p. 175.

[105]"What about the Middle Class? A Lay Sermon," *Daily Citizen*, 19 October 1912; see *Shaw: 'The Chucker-Out'*, p. 217.

[106]His friends in the theater came under a particularly heavy barrage of allusions to Dickens. He enjoined Gilbert Murray, for example, after a performance of Murray's *Andromache*, to "want people trained to speak and move handsomely,

and to strike the chords of the human heart feelingly enough to touch Mr Guppy." As Shaw well knew, Mr. Guppy is the repulsive young clerk in the office of Kenge and Carboy of *Bleak House,* who falls in love with Esther Summerson, but is of course refused. Shaw slyly planted his own Mr. Guppy in a brief playlet, "Beauty's Duty," tossed off in an idle moment in 1913. Here Shaw erects a situation in which a young client (Horace) seeks advice from his equally young solicitor about divorcing a wife who insists on exercising her astounding talent of improving men by making them fall in love with her. The conversation drifts back and forth as the solicitor suggests alternatives and urges his client against taking drastic action. At the close of the playlet, the solicitor's junior clerk, a Mr. Guppy, enters the room clearly dazzled and bubbling over with barely suppressed emotion. Horace immediately deduces that his wife is in the outer office, where she has been practicing her wiles. On that cryptic note the playlet concludes.
Letter to Gilbert Murray, in *Collected Letters: 1898–1910,* p. 222 (15 March 1901); "Beauty's Duty," in *Collected Plays with their Prefaces,* VII, 613–16.

Editors' Note

All of Shaw's principal commentaries on Charles Dickens, as well as significant extracts from his lectures, critical essays, reviews, and private correspondence are collected in this volume. Although it results in some duplication of Shaw's ideas and opinions, we have designedly retained the recurrent elements to enable the reader to determine the degree of consistency of narrative and phraseology over the years, and to note the shifts of emphasis, the emergence of new details, the submergence of earlier ones, and the dramatizations, shadings, and embroiderings.

We have, where necessary, corrected typographical errors, faulty punctuation, and Shaw's occasional misspellings of the names of the Dickens characters, notably Betsy [Betsey] Trotwood, Jo [Joe] Gargery, Mrs. Macstinger [MacStinger], and Trabbs's [Trabb's] boy. We have italicized titles of books and journals and set off with quotation marks titles of short works where Shaw has failed to do so; but have otherwise reproduced the published and unpublished writings as originally styled, retaining Shaw's idiosyncratic spelling and punctuation in those texts over which he had authorial or editorial control.

The pseudonymously signed review, "Wellerisms," and the unsigned review, "The Pickwick Pantomime," have been identified by references in Shaw's as yet unpublished shorthand diaries.

From the inception of this book down to its galley proofing we have benefited from the insight and the patient labors of Philip Winsor. To him, and to Evander Lomke, of the Frederick Ungar Publishing Company, we offer our deepest thanks.

We acknowledge with much gratitude an indebtedness for valuable research or textual assistance to Leonard N. Beck (Subject Collections Specialist, Library of Congress), Sir James Pitman, Gordon N. Ray, Edgar Rosenberg, Barbara Smoker, the late Leslie C.

Staples, Stanley Weintraub, and the reference staffs of the University of Guelph Library, the San Antonio Public Library, and the Pennsylvania State University Libraries at University Park and the Beaver Campus. Our thanks also to Shirley Rader for her generosity in typing the manuscript of the introduction.

Permission to publish Shaw manuscripts and correspondence from their collections has kindly been provided by the following institutions: British Library (manuscript of the fragmentary "From Dickens to Ibsen" and a note by Shaw concerning correspondence with Kate Perugini); Cornell University Library (letters to Gerald Gould, Kate Perugini, and Gladys Storey, in the Bernard F. Burgunder Shaw Collection); Humanities Research Center of the University of Texas at Austin (letters to St. John Ervine, Anmer Hall, Hugh Kingsmill, and Sir William B. Nicoll, and an annotated proof of the title page to *Great Expectations* (1937), together with Shaw's drawing of Pip); New York Public Library, Astor, Lenox and Tilden Foundations (letters to Merle Armitage, Frank S. Johnson, and Clement K. Shorter, in the Henry W. and Albert A. Berg Collection).

D.H.L.

M.Q.

Shaw
on
Dickens

PART I

Principal Criticisms

Wellerisms

Satirical review of C. F. Rideal and Charles Kent's *"Wellerisms" from "Pickwick" and "Master Humphrey's Clock,"* pseudonymously signed "By the Rev. C. W. Stiggins, Junr., of Box Hill" (the Rev. Mr. Stiggins in *Pickwick Papers* is an intemperate, hypocritical minister to a fanatical congregation). *Pall Mall Gazette* (London), 15 April 1887.

In detaching the utterances of the elder and younger Weller from the attractive framework in which Dickens presented them, the authors of this little book have rendered a service to English morality. That two men, illiterate, intolerant, sensual, ribald, and unseemly, should be idolized in the nineteenth century, merely because their solutions of the most pressing problems of life were so inadequate as to be irresistibly ludicrous, is a strong argument against the modern fashion of encouraging from the pulpit the national habit of novel reading. The old but unreverend Anthony Weller, who, though well-to-do in his station, drove his son into the streets to shift for himself when very young; who, though himself so gross a feeder and tippler that he was called "Corpulence" in his own family, yet sneered at women for drinking tea, and brutally assaulted the guest who trespassed on his hospitality for a glass of pine-apple rum; who, whilst cowering before the woman who craved some better spiritual food than perpetual Wellerisms, forced a bout at fisticuffs upon a man greatly inferior to him in weight, and rendered incapable of self-defence by the machinations of two confederates who drove coaches to Oxford, and were experts in all disgraceful practices ("two friends o' mine as works the Oxford road, and is up to all kinds o' games"—see page 77); who never attended a place of worship or (assuming him to have been an Agnostic) a scientific lecture—this unnatural father and ignorant and greedy scoffer, coward, and bully has outlived the toleration which his absurdity and the low ethical standard of his day gained him for a time.

Of Samuel Weller it need only be said that he was his father's son. He had the gutter point of honour—to have a humiliating repartee for all comers, the pothouse accomplishment of skill and readiness as a pugilist, and the true outcast-class instinct to resist officers of the law and prevaricate in the witness-box (see The

Queen v. Pickwick and Tupman, Bardell v. Pickwick, and the disgraceful Boldwig affair). His fidelity to his master is accounted for by the fact that he could not have changed his place except for a worse one. That he had no real faith in Mr. Pickwick is shown by his evil construction of the mistake about the bedroom in the Ipswich hotel, and his instantaneous conviction of the justice of Mrs. Bardell's case, which he nevertheless did not hesitate to damage in court to the utmost of his power (see pages 19, 35, 84, etc.) Of honesty he seems to have had no conception; for he admits without apparent shame that when he wanted anything he asked for it in a respectful and obliging manner; but, if refused, took it, lest he should be led to do anything wrong through not having it— an explanation which proves that he was conscious of a murderous disposition in himself. In certain matters he was truthful: his disregard of the feelings of others and his indifference to their opinion of him led him to be frank on occasions when a more sensitive man would have been reticent; but as to his allegations concerning the young nobleman and the parlour door, the gentleman in difficulties, the parrot, the soldier whose evidence Mr. Justice Stareleigh properly declined to admit, the gentleman on the right side of the garden wall, the Lord Mayor and the Chief Secretary of State, the King dissolving the Parliament, the peer who obtained a pension, and other persons far outside the sphere of a valet who had graduated as a waggoner's boy, no one who has critically examined these will hesitate to reject them as fictions. They are probably not even original: a retentive memory, and the narrator's inordinate love of displaying his sharpness before an audience, sufficiently account for their introduction. There is absolutely no historical authority for the saying attributed to Richard III. (page 42). Even that "extensive and peculiar knowledge of London" which has been so much insisted on by Wellerolators shrinks on examination to a chance acquaintance with a peculiarity in one of the tables in a certain public-house. Of the treasure-houses of science and art in the metropolis, its temples, and its hallowed relics, he knew nothing. He was, in fact, at best a liar, a thief, a ruffian, and an ignoramus; and the sooner the foolish fashion of admiring him is dropped, the better for the tone of English society.

The Wellers were probably not indigenous Londoners. Comparative philology suggests rather a German Jewish origin for the family. (See p. 80, "Put it down a we, my lord," and other locutions of the same kind.)

From Dickens to Ibsen

Hitherto unpublished fragment of an essay begun on 1 November 1889 and abandoned at the end of that month. Shaw's views on Ibsen were expressed the following year in a paper read before the Fabian Society that became the basis for *The Quintessence of Ibsenism* (1891).

A novel or a play has two aspects, the documentary and the artistic. A book of the highest documentary value may remain unread for want of artistic handling: example, a blue book [i.e., an official government report]. A book written with delightful art may leave its many readers no wiser—save in so far as to be happier is to be wiser—than before for want of any documentary character: example, a fairy tale. There are people who protest against the documentary element in works of literary art on the ground that art should not be didactic, because it exists solely for its own sake. There are also people who declare that the value of such works is purely documentary, because the art is valuable solely for its efficacy in spreading the documentary content more widely. These are deficient, one in the appetite for knowledge, the other in the appetite for beauty; and their wranglings are such as might arise between a blind musician and a deaf painter over the comparative merits of a beautifully designed musical instrument which could not be put in tune, and an ugly one with a divine tone and perfect intonation. The greatest man is the completest man, he whose eyes are as good as his ears, and his head as his hands. The inferiority of Monticelli to Raphael is not so much the inferiority of one painter to another as the difference between a more or less completely wise man; and the same may be said of the difference between Mr Swinburne and Goethe, Canova and Praxiteles, M. Gounod and Wagner. Mr Robert Buchanan and Ibsen.[1] No analytical critic will

---

[1]Adolphe Monticelli (1824–86) was a French painter of swirling, dreamlike scenes of courtly revels, whose work was much admired by van Gogh. Antonio Canova (1757–1822), Italian sculptor of papal tombs and statues of Napoleon, Princess Borghese (as "Venus Victrix"), and George Washington, was a leading exponent of Neoclassicism. Praxiteles (fl. 370–30 B.C.) was the greatest Attic sculptor of his age; his "Aphrodite of Cnidus" was considered by Pliny the Elder to be the finest statue in the world. Robert Buchanan (1841–1901), British poet and novelist, enemy of the pre-Raphaelites, was a virulent anti-Ibsenite as well.

contend that the members of these pairs stand as far apart as eminent artists as they obviously do as great men. If, instead of comparing Mr Swinburne with Goethe, we compare him with Byron, Mr Swinburne himself will be able to prove easily that he is the greater artist of the two. It does not follow—and to avoid digressive controversy arising in the reader's mind I offer no opinion on the point—that he is the greater man. Transferring the comparison from the men to their works, it may be expressed thus:—that the greatest work is not so much the greatest artistic feat as the greatest lesson, revelation, illuminant, or, to use the term already introduced, the greatest document. When Andrea del Sarto, in Mr Browning's poem, takes a piece of chalk, and corrects Raphael's drawing, he does so only to console himself for a moment with an infinitesimal set-off to his own inferiority. When Mozart, in real life, added a strain of wonderful harmony to "The people that walked in darkness," the increase in the total value of the *Messiah* was not as much as a millionth per cent: we are anxious to discard it in our mere dislike to suffer any meddling whatever with a great original.

The discrimination between artistic and documentary in art work, leads to a corresponding discrimination in criticism between description, or the attempt to make the reader imagine how beautiful a work is, and comment on or discussion of the documentary side of it. The first is a fine art in itself, and is too expensive to enter largely into the common or journalistic criticism. When it is badly done, it is excessively dull. Documentary criticism can be taken at any level according to the capacity of the critic, and made fairly interesting, as it ranges from mere news to pure philosophy—from the concert notice or "analytic programme" to Aristotle, Lessing, Schopenhauer & Wagner. From every new level a new documentary criticism is possible. In the case of Dickens and Ibsen, all the documentary criticism available from the level of the middle class literary man has already been offered. It may be summed up in the two common remarks that Dickens, as the Chief Butler said of Mr Merdle after his suicide, "never was the Gentleman," and that "no woman would walk out of the house and leave her children there, like Nora in *The Doll's House*." One is a gentlemanly criticism and the other a ladylike one; but I will anticipate here so far as to say that Dickens's documents belong to the struggle of Man for social equality: Ibsen's, to the struggle of Woman for individual liberty. My own qualification for producing fresh criticism of both is that, though formally a middle class literary man, I am, from the middle class point of view, an enemy of religion and society: that is, I regard atheism as the first condition of true religion; I abhor the British family as an institution which degrades women and imposes their degradation as a blight on the whole social harvest; and I make no distinction whatever between the economic position of a gentleman of property and that of a thief. Such a self introduction as this is not yet customary; but since Shelley's time such people as are likely to take up a magazine article have become accustomed to meet atheists and socialists without shying and bolting; and my interpretation of two great writers may be interesting, either as example or warning, to many who may deplore my views as sincerely as I deplore theirs. Deploring is a form of persecution; but it is not lethal, and so remains for the present within the bounds of civility.

Charles Dickens was born into a false position as a member of the shabby genteel class—the class which pretends to gentility without the means to support its pretension. When, in a severe pecuniary strait, he was sent to work among boys of the laboring class at bottlewashing, he felt bitterly disgraced and degraded; and his refusal to continue it was submitted to as morally valid by his family, except his mother, whom he never forgave for this: all his boy heroes, without exception, are orphans; and all the mothers in his books are either silly (Mrs Nickleby and Mrs Copperfield) or their son's worst enemies (Mrs Steerforth and Mrs Clennam). Betsey Trotwood and Betty Higden are not the mothers of the boys for whom they do all that a woman can do out of pity and affection for a child. And when Dickens, with his utterly ungentlemanly and entirely right and noble instinct for placing his most intimate concerns before his fellowmen instead of locking them up as skeletons in the family solicitor's cupboard, made his will a public document as he had made his separation from his wife a public matter, the claim advanced in that will for the respect and gratitude of his children was not made on behalf of their mother, but of their aunt.

Here, then, is a huge omission from the middle class family

point of view in Dickens's works—the omission of the maternal superstition. But it is not a reasoned omission, nor in its manner of execution a just one. The fact that he resented his own mother's action shews that he believed to the end that she *ought* to have suffered increased poverty to preserve in him a sense of dignity, essentially unsocial and false, of which her own hard experiences had probably by that time made her impatient. He does not appear to have seen that the family system, especially among people clinging to appearances with straitened means, sacrifices the whole life and individuality of the woman to the struggle to keep her children fed, taught, patched, and darned; and that there is no foundation for the assumption that the blood relationship will create such a degree of interest and affection between mother and child as to make this monstrous obligation a pleasure. Neither in this nor in any other matter did Dickens ever catch the woman's point of view, or escape from that of the British bourgeois. To him the perfect woman is simply the perfect domestic convenience. Great as was his advance in insight and comprehension both before and after *Bleak House*, the jingling of Esther Summerson's housekeeping keys fulfilled his conception of feminine music to the last.

When Dickens became an attorney's clerk his point of social honor was satisfied. He was free of fustian and corduroy—of the "working class." He ranked with Messrs Dodson and Fogg's gentlemen, not with Josiah Bounderby's "hands." If, when considering the studies he gives us in *Pickwick* of his peers, we bear in mind that the artisan class in London had produced between 183[0] and 18[60] men who had deliberately incurred two years rigorous imprisonment for the sake of freedom of the press by volunteering to sell unstamped publications, we are tempted for a moment to doubt the instincts of a youth who threw in his lot with the cads to escape the contamination of the heroes. But account must be taken of Dickens's knowledge that his tool was the pen and not the saw or the spade, and of his ignorance of the existence of the heroes. He knew nothing about the working classes except that they were poor; and as he had suffered from poverty himself more than from anything else, he was filled with the true middle class pity for them—the pity that is not sympathy because it is not informed by any knowledge of how the working classes think and live and take their poverty.

It is true that to be a human being, especially a male human being, was to be a thing concerning which Dickens knew a good deal; but it cannot be said that Dickens's genius enabled him to know the working classes because he knew men, and wage workers, if their class characteristics be abstracted, are but men like the rest of us. Dickens indeed had the special shabby genteel disadvantage of a false knowledge of the working class based on his childish observation of and intimacy with domestic servants, who have hardly any class characteristic but their illiteracy in common with the workers who, in mine, factory, workshop, and East End quarter, live their own life, obeying the factory bell at stated hours intead of the drawingroom bell at all hours, and getting its glimpses of a better life through the imagination instead of through the keyhole. All Dickens's earlier successes in working class portraiture are types of the workers whose occupation bring them in contact with middle class men. There are domestic servants of both sexes, coachmen, and monthly nurses, but, save for one absurd engine driver [Mr. Toodle] in *Dombey and Son*, not one normal representative of the great mass who are not on speaking terms with respectability. Simon Tappertit, whose historical period is before the industrial revolution, is as much a creature of the kitchen as Miggs herself. There is no pretence of realism about Mr Peggotty and his son: Peggotty herself is credible; and so is Mrs Gummidge; but the rest of the family are as purely romantic as the heroes of Don Quixote's favorite books. In *Bleak House* the humours of Chancery Lane district—of Mrs Piper and Mrs Perkins and the child [Johnny Piper] that knew not fear[—]can all be observed by a shabby genteel boy in the kitchen and in the streets.

Dickens, then, did not at first know the masses. And he was equally at a loss with the classes, for want of secondary education. His immense instinct for letters saved him from illiteracy; but just as many men of great capacity, with the best accessible intellectual training and equipment, remain illiterate to the end of their lives for want of this instinct, expressing themselves, if at all, only by symbols and diagrams accompanied by a few bald and clumsy verbal references; so a born writer, however ignorant, is able to make such an artistic word play round any subject that only experts perceive when he knows nothing about it. Now Dickens did not, like Bulwer Lytton, habitually use his literary dexterity to pass off mere smattering as scholarship.[2] But if his honesty had not prevented him he would still have been saved by the fact that he was not even a smatterer in the arts and sciences. Bulwer knew that there were bodies of inferences, coordinated into more or less complete syntheses, and systematized as law, philosophy, ethics, physics, metaphysics and so on. He had got the hang of them, and, by eking out what he knew with fictitious but appropriate detail, could give them their place as social factors in his novels. Disraeli had the same illumination; and it is this which distinguishes Bulwer and Disraeli so remarkably from Thackeray and Dickens; for Thackeray, from want of university aptitude, was almost as uneducated as Dickens was from want of opportunity. If Bulwer and Disraeli, instead of being, as novelists, a pair of romantic humbugs, had had the sincerity of Thackeray and the inspiration of Dickens, we might have had a novelist like Jean Paul Richter[3] and a school of writers of the stamp of Paul Heyse[4] instead of the adventurous schoolboy romances and smart barristerial criticism of middle class drawing-room life on which we batten at present. Dickens, however, was not merely ignorant of "the humanities": he was absolutely unconscious of them. Just as a church organ blower considers religion finally disposed of by his discovery that the clergyman is a hypocrite, so it is impossible to read Dickens's early works without seeing that he considered politics, jurisprudence and natural science disposed of by his discovery, as a reporter, that the average member of parliament, judge, serjeant at law, or member of a learned society was a social *non valeur*, nay, worse, a disutility, a nuisance. So long as science was represented in his mind by Professor Swosser[5] and the gentleman who mistook Mr Pickwick's lantern for a

---

[2]Edward Bulwer-Lytton (1802–73), 1st Baron Lytton of Knebworth, novelist and dramatist, wrote such popular historical/romantic novels as *The Last Days of Pompeii* (1834) and *Rienzi* (1835).

[3]Jean Paul Richter (1763–1825), German humorist, wrote fantasy novels that had a wide vogue.

[4]Paul von Heyse (1830–1914), German author of realist novels and plays, won the Nobel Prize for Literature, 1910.

[5]Shaw here confusedly conflated the first two spouses of the thrice-married Mrs. Bayham Badger: Captain Swosser of the Royal Navy and Professor Dingo, in *Bleak House*.

meteor [in Chapter 39] and had his head knocked "with a hollow sound" against the stable door by Sam Weller, he could not take science seriously. Observe, in this connection, that he made the missing distinction in one case. He expressly pointed out in the case of Stiggins that his ridicule of the preacher was not ridicule of religion. But he never dreamt of pointing out that the ridicule which he heaped on other professors was equally without prejudice to the arts and sciences which they professed; nor had he an idea of dwarfing his pedants by exhibiting their pettiness against a background of the vast scopes in which they were meddling, as Goethe did in *Faust* when he too portrayed a "scientific gentleman" in Wagner. He knew as little of the great world of thought as he did of the great world of labor. Of the two main natural castes in English society, the picked men of the artisan class and the picked men of the highly educated professional class he knew only what came to him by what Nicholas Rowe, in an exquisitely ridiculous apology for Shakespear's small Latin and less Greek, called "a mere light of Nature."[6] And though, to hazard another quotation—this time from Mr Montague Tigg—"Nature's nobs feel for Nature's nobs the world over," Dickens failed in sympathy for the trained intellect because his extraordinary ready made power of observation kept his imagination too busy to admit of his cultivating his undeveloped powers of abstraction and co-ordination.

Another commercial class disability of his lay in the fact that though he was a born artist he never thought of seeking satisfaction for his sense of beauty in things which had any other use. He felt the pathos of autumn, the mystery of evening, the gloom of winter and night; but he did not suffer from Philistine curtains and furniture or from flashy scarves and watchchains as Mr William Morris did; and the literary form of *Sketches by Boz* and *Pickwick*, though enormously funny, would have made de Quinc[e]y or Coleridge writhe with lacerated sense of grace. The style, when it has any original artistic character at all, is either whimsical for comic effect or, in tragic or sentimental passages, all but deliberately metrical. What it is when it takes an artistic character that is not original may be seen in the following passage:

[6]Preface to Rowe's edition of Shakespeare's plays (six volumes, 1709).

[The passage, not identified by Shaw in his draft, presumably was to be drawn from the impassioned scene between Nicholas and Ralph Nickleby in Chapter 20 of *Nicholas Nickleby*.]

A few chapters later, the pages are crammed with ridicule of the theatrical diction of Crummles and Mr Lenville, though not one of their speeches is more stagey than this put by Dickens into the mouth of his hero.

Under all these disadvantages Dickens produced *Pickwick*, *Oliver Twist*, *Nicholas Nickleby* and *The Old Curiosity Shop*. Compared to such masterpieces as *Little Dorrit* and *Great Expectations*, they are what the *Comedy of Errors* is to *The Tempest* or *Love's Labour's Lost* to *King Lear*, what Beethoven's septuor is to the ninth symphony or [Wagner's] *Rienzi* to *Parsifal*. But in them his secondary education begins. He thought over the New Poor Law, over debtors' prisons and imprisonment for debt, and over boy farming in Yorkshire schools. Then he saw a man hung and thought over capital punishment. Then he dipped into the scepticisms of Chesterfield and Larochefoucauld, and made a historical study for *Barnaby Rudge*. Finally, he went to America, and saw society, the contemporary cockney phase of which he had hitherto considered as coextensive with civilization except as to its purely national traits, at a stage of evolution that was quite new to him. His descriptions of such of the phenomena as he had eyes for are of the highest value: his interpretation of them could hardly be shallower. The American scenes in *Martin Chuzzlewit* have all the intellectual crudity of his first phase. Intellectual digestion is a slow process even with men who have been trained to it; and the American food was too recently swallowed. The English part of the book is the first work of his middle period. Pecksniff, the typical middle-class Englishman, was terrible. The laughter at him was hollow and uneasy: the circulation fell off at once from the huge *Nickleby* standard; the effort to make believe that Pecksniff was somebody else was too irksome. But there was no need for this national discomfiture. It is not the evil will in Pecksniff that is typical: it is his form only—his ways and manners and ideals of respectability. Leave the formal Pecksniff unchanged, substituting only a good will for the evil one; and you at once have Micawber. Take Pecksniff, evil will and all, changing only his sex; and you have Mrs General.

Leave the formal Mrs General unchanged, substituting, as before, only a good will for the evil one; and you have [Miss Twinkleton] the little schoolmistress in *Edwin Drood* who read novels aloud to her pupil, not as she found them written, but as she thought they ought to have been written in the interests of middle class morals. For all that, Pecksniff was terrible, because he brought into relief the cardinal sin of the middle class, Hypocrisy. Middle class prosperity was based upon working class poverty. So was upper class prosperity; but the upper class did not blink the fact: they either justified it as part of a divinely appointed order, or cynically accepted their luck as such without pretending to justify it. Besides, there is "no damned nonsense of personal merit" about the Garter[7]: a Duke, since his nobility cannot be challenged, can be as rude or as shabbily dressed as he likes, whereas the commercial or professional gentleman must wear his uniform of silk hat and starched linen, and go through his drill of company manners on pain of ostracism; so that successive Lord Mayors of London are surprised to find that the genuine aristocratic tone, instead of being middle class respectability in its supreme manifestation, is a sort of free and easy rowdyism which sits easily on no outsiders except poet laureates and vagrants. Most tradesmen are at a loss in speaking to a lord: most successful prizefighters catch the correct tone in ten minutes.

This obligation to dress and behave fashionably is only an application of the general Protestant obligation to be personally righteous, moral, religious, and thus earn the divine right to respectability which the chance of birth had failed to win. This involved the claim that this was the only right really divine; that rank was but the guinea's stamp; that true hearts are more than coronets—in short, that the pretensions of the feudal class had no moral validity. And this had to be reconciled somehow with incorrigible envy of the feudal class; with intriguing to intermarry with them; with bragging of twentieth cousinships with them; with every presentable sort of tufthunting. Further, the divine right of individual merit, being republican and open to all, carried with it no moral authority to rob and harry the poor. Yet it had to be

[7]William Lamb (1779–1848), 2nd Viscount Melbourne, is credited with having said, "I like the [Order of] the Garter; there's no damned merit in it."

reconciled with such atrocious pillage of and cruelty to the proletariat that socialistic laws had to be made to protect at least the infants of the poor from the horrors of the uninspected and unregulated factory and mine; and to this day we are looking on at respectable middle class men in [a] Cannon St hotel savagely howling down a benevolent woman who asked them to sacrifice some of their nine per cent in order that their employees might be away from home for less than sixteen hours a day, and get a little more than four shillings for it. No such reconciliation being possible, the middle classes had only two alternatives: to relinquish their riches or to pretend that there was no contradiction to be reconciled. Choosing the latter, they built up a gigantic hypocrisy, lie upon lie, keeping up the credit of the false coin by always passing it among themselves as genuine, and nailing down genuine gold to the counter, besides punishing its utterers as impudent smashers. In order to justify their cringing to the aristocracy it was only necessary to invest every aristocrat with high personal merit, and then to pay proper respect to that merit, worshipping, not the coronet and the Norman blood, but the true heart and the simple faith which they placed gratuitously to the credit of every titled person who would speak of them as "my friend" at a public meeting or to them by any term at a private one. All this was not to be done without constant and anxious hushing-up, without muzzling of the press, the police, and of themselves. But it was a trifle compared to the monstrous labor of justifying their insolence to and oppression of the poor by investing them with personal demerit, and exhibiting their poverty as the just effect of improvidence, sexual incontinence, drunkenness and squalor. Those of them who had more than enough to live luxuriously on[,] saved capital, and then pretended that "thrift," being an abstract virtue, was equally easy to people with less than half enough to purchase the bare necessaries of life. They abolished favoritism and patronage in the professions and public services, fenced these in with arduous competitive examinations as guarantees of individual merit, and then pretended that these professions and services were as "open" to the son of the laborer brutalized by heavy manual compulsory toil from his early boyhood, as to their own sons upon whose education in public school, university or crammer's boarding house money had been lavished up to the moment of examination. They gave the working man his vote, and then pretended that he could elect whom he pleased, taking care at the same time that nobody without a thousand pounds loose cash and an independent income could think of a seat in parliament as within his means. This they did— this "damned compact Liberal majority," as Ibsen called them; and the result was that they became so defiled and corrupted by the poison of their own perpetual shamming that at last self seeking, hypocrisy, and the keeping and cooking of debtor and creditor accounts in personal merit became natural to them. The environment of falsehood had modified the organism, and the species Pecksniff was the result. And Dickens, with his keen eye and his great heart, saw Pecksniff, felt him, and fell on him with all his might. From that time forward story telling was no longer his end: it was only his weapon. All the rest of his work is war on the classes.

It must not be supposed that he attained complete consciousness of this at one flash. Pecksniff was conceived by him, not as a typical middle class man, but as one of those detestable individuals on whose occurrence he so strongly insisted.

Hence we have Rigaud, Carker, Murdstone and their like. But the association, in Pecksniff's case, of a wicked spirit with the characteristic modes of thought and life of the "respectable" middle class shews that he instinctively felt in those modes of thought and life an atmosphere of darkness and fraud in which no honest man's soul could thrive. And as he elaborated the details of the portrait, and warmed to his work, he must have become more and more aware that the natural scoundrelism of Pecksniff was a superfluous element in his plan. The mere facts that he had no ability as an architect, and could not have obtained the social status which he naturally desired except as a "professional" man, were quite sufficient to explain why, mainly through the fault of the class system, he thought it better to be a sham architect than no architect at all, that sham being the "dram of eale"[8] (as Shakspere says in the "hopelessly corrupt" passage which everybody understands) which corrupted him all through. But he was not a sham among honest

[8]*Hamlet*, I.iv.36.

men. Every middle class man who is not exceptionally gifted is bound, if he would be respectable, not only to refuse intercourse on equal terms to nine out of ten of his fellow citizens, but to do so on the ground that intercourse with them would contaminate him, he being the superior person. And sham virtue is by no means less poisonous than sham skill in architecture. That was only the particular form in which the general sham happened to impose itself on poor Pecksniff.

Accordingly in the next book, *Dombey and Son*, the middle class is typified by Mr Dombey, a man not at all malevolent, who, having no originality and little imagination or sympathy, accepts the false dignity and the false ambition imposed on him by society, and maintains and pursues them dutifully as best he can. This negativeness of character prevents him from standing out as a tragic figure; but the book is the tragedy of his life. First the utter invalidity of the whole social scheme of which he is the victim is brought into relief by his inability to explain it to his little poet son, who has originality, imagination and sympathy. "What is money?" says Paul to his father; and his father, called upon to justify the god of the middle class, breaks down and is confounded out of the mouth of a babe and suckling. Then, having no other conception of education than grinding a child into a middle class man, he sends his boy to the most respectable and exclusive mill he can find. The result is that the child is ground to death. The middle class could not see that the tragedy here was the tragedy of the father. They snivelled abundantly over little Paul, and a drawingroom ballad "What are the wild waves say-ay-ing, Sister, the whole day-ay long" had an immense vogue among them.

The second part of the book consists of a startlingly explicit exposure of the one institution in the purity and moral respectability of its form of which the middle class specially prides itself—the institution of marriage. Mr Dombey, having as the middle class father sacrificed his son in the customary effort to make him a mere money hunter, now, as the middle class widower with money made in trade, proceeds to purchase a wife who will connect him with the aristocracy. Dickens's method of pointing out that this typical proceeding is a deliberate act of prostitution is the most extreme he could have adopted. He confronts the lady and her mother [Edith and Mrs. Skewton] with a miserable street thief whose daughter is a common harlot ["Good" Mrs. Brown and Alice "Marwood"]; and he shews the moral identity of the positions of the two couples in a terrible scene which ends with the old lady joining the old procuress in a whining complaint of the ingratitude of the two daughters, who rebel fiercely against the degradation from which neither can see any escape. The bargain, however, is concluded in due course; and is followed by the assemblies in Mr Dombey's drawingroom, where his wife's friends of the aristocratic set get together at one end of the room, leaving his own commercial set to digest the snubbing at the other. Finally the woman whom he bought—just as he might have only hired her had their relative rank been reversed—disgraces him by eloping with a rascal who robs and ruins him. He survives the total shipwreck, and, not being naturally a bad man, finds himself happy for the first time in this life with the burden of his social position off his shoulders. Nobody dared to propose that Dickens should be prosecuted for this book—in fact, class society was too dense to feel the full force of the attack; but the general verdict was that there was a great falling off in Dickens. And so there was—a falling off from his own class, which he had now thoroughly found out.

He now turned from society to the individual for a while. *Dombey and Son* had led him to make a study of his own earliest experiences for the poet child Paul Dombey. The book did not exhaust either the subject or its fascination for him; and he pursued it in *David Copperfield*, which is for the greater part a romantic autobiography. It is a book of pain, doubt, anxiety, and unfulfilment. The figures are half laborious unachieved studies from life, half dream figures; and they pass in a panoramic show which at last fades out and is formally announced as closed by a formal winding up which is as conventional as the playing of God Save the Queen at an illusionist's entertainment. David Copperfield, lifelike as a child and as a young man, never achieves complete manhood and self realization. Dickens could describe himself as a boy: he could not understand himself as a man. He has only dealt seriously with one phase of his adult life—the failure and disillusion of his marriage. There is a remarkable combination of tenderness and ruthlessness in the picture of Dora. She is made to appear utterly worthless and useless, so incorrigibly silly and spoiled, that Kant himself would have denied her the right of an individual to be considered as an end rather than as a means, and would have admitted that her death was an inevitable consequence of the absence of any mortal reason why she should live. But after all Dora's failure is only a failure from the point of view which judges the daughter of a Queen's proctor solely by her fitness to act as housekeeper, head nurserymaid and odalisque to a professional gentleman. As an odalisque, Dora was a success; and it was in fact that very success which, until it palled, blinded David to her incapacity as his housekeeper. The moral which Betsey Trotwood draws about "unsuitability" may be the practical moral for a young professional man about to marry; but it is not the true moral of Dora; and that Dickens had not reached the true moral is shewn by the introduction of another young lady named Agnes, who is offered as being in general terms everything that Dora was not, and who is decidedly the most seventh rate heroine ever produced by a first rate artist. In the equally unsatisfactory character of Wickfield, there is a faint attempt to deal with the inadequacy of the proposal to explain human action by "motives"; but Dickens was no Schopenhauer, and he could get no further with the problem than an incomplete sketch of a man entirely losing his will through adopting the motive theory. Rosa Dartle, the woman whose egotism is of the insane type, and whose whole stock of affection, instead of being healthily diffused, is concentrated cruelly and furiously upon one selfish hero who has disfigured her with a blow from a hammer, is a vivid study from life, not yet related in the author's mind. Steerforth is a notable advance upon the conventional *jeune premier* Nicholas Nickleby; but many less gifted novelists than Dickens were already protesting against the hero-worship of the handsome, selfish, wilful young man. Dickens had begun the protest like the rest by setting up against him the clumsy, shy, plain, kindhearted duffer, Tom Pinch versus Martin Chuzzlewit, [Dobbin] versus George Osborne,[9] the plain governess versus the beautiful but vicious heiress; but that elementary phase is passed in *David Copperfield*: there is no attempt to disparage Steerforth's

[9]William Dobbin, in Thackeray's *Vanity Fair*, is the long-suffering, patient admirer of Amelia Sedley, widow of the unfaithful George Osborne.

address by a glorification of awkwardness, or his beauty by a praise of plainness: he is condemned solely for his criminal want of consideration for others. To all these themes—the Rosa Dartle, the Dora, and the Steerforth, Dickens returned later on, when he had followed them up further. Postponing further consideration of them to that point, it is only necessary to say, as far as *David Copperfield* is concerned, that the Peggotties are as factitious as Dickens's genius allowed him to make them; that the comic interludes of the humors of Micawber at last become mere mechanical repetitions of the same trick of verbiage; and that the little sally at the end about model prisons shew[s] Dickens as still void of a comprehensive view of the social question with which, for the space of this book, he had called a truce.

In *Bleak House* he gets back to it, having stumbled upon a tremendous mare's nest in the Court of Chancery. That institution is a derived evil, not a fundamental one. Given our property system and our system of inheritance; and the Court of Chancery is inevitable. Where the carcass is, there will the eagles be gathered together. As long as the owner of an estate remains a mere parasite upon the tenantry, swallowing up so much of the fruit of their labor every year without rendering them any equivalent, it matters little to them whether the parasite is Miss Flite, or Jarndyce, or the man from Shropshire, or Conversation Kenge, with his bill of costs. Indeed, the swallowing up of an estate in costs is by far the most satisfactory ending of a chancery suit, since the parties who get it have had to do at least some sort of professional work for it. This does not seem to have struck Dickens. When Proudhon examined the individualist synthesis of political economy as completed by Ricardo,[10] he said in effect:—"Gentlemen: I have to draw your serious attention to the fact that this science, instead of providing a justification of property, is a *reductio ad absurdum* of it—that property is, in brief, theft." The "rights" of which the Court of Chancery defrauds suitors are generally everybody else's wrongs: they, too, are a *reductio ad absurdum* of our whole system of vested

[10]Pierre-Joseph Proudhon (1809–65), French Socialist-anarchist politician, was a critic of all extant forms of political organization. David Ricardo (1772–1823), English economist, was the author of *Principles of Political Economy and Taxation* (1817).

rights in the spoliation of the industrious by the idle. Dickens gives no hint of what Cobbett,[11] in his "Advice to Young Men," had pointed out long before, that the expectation of property, the hope of stepping into dead men's shoes and trampling with them live men's backs, is what demoralizes men. The virtuous John Jarndyce gives Richard Carstone abundant warnings that he will be disappointed in winning the suit: he never tells him the plain truth that all the properties in the world would not absolve him from the moral obligation to earn his own livelihood by his own exertions. Just so do we hear bishops warning young men not to gamble on the ground that they will probably lose, but never whispering a word of the real objection to gambling—i.e., that it is dishonest because it is an attempt to get money without earning it. However, the discovery of the rottenness of the Court of Chancery was an important instalment of the exposure of the great middle class sham begun in *Dombey and Son.*

In that book, by the way, there is an aristocrat—Cousin Feenix—from whose futility Dickens made the important reservation that he had "the heart of a gentleman." A renewed tenderness towards the upper class is not an uncommon effect of the finding out of the middle class. In *Bleak House* we find this view pursued in the elaborate portrait of Sir Leicester Dedlock, who, arrogant numskull as he is, has nothing of Pecksniff or Dombey about him. Dickens had not discovered the peculiar brutality of the country gentleman: he sees Sir Leicester with the eyes of a cockney. Chesney Wold[12] is much more like Holland Park than like a real country house, with the agricultural laborer and his wages always round the corner. But the political tone of the country family interest, and the desperate boredom of country splendor is shewn with a fidelity that is all the more convincing because there is now no bitterness in it. For by this time the deeper and deeper feeling which marked Dickens's advance as a writer had become almost continuous in his books. In *Pickwick* there is no tenderness, even in the tragic touches. From *Nickleby* to *Martin Chuzzlewit* the serious parts are

[11]William Cobbett (1763–1835), English journalist and politician, was a champion of radicalism.
[12]Chesney Wold, a stately country home in *Bleak House*, was modelled after Rockingham Castle, Northamptonshire.

combative and resentful: we have such scenes as old Weller kicking Stiggins, Nicholas caning Squeers, old Chuzzlewit hammering Pecksniff with a knobby stick. But Carker is struck down by an impersonal fate instead of having his head punched by Captain Cuttle; David Copperfield's worst humiliation is the blow to which Uriah Heep provokes him; and no bodily violence is offered to Mr Smallweed or Mr Vholes, though if the latter had by ill fortune strayed into *Nicholas Nickleby*, he would certainly have ended in a horse pond. The old street boy tendency to laugh at grotesque people without thinking any further about them vanishes in *Bleak House*. Micawber was the last of the list of people in whom Dickens could see only butts for his fun. Mr Guppy and Mr Jobling are not very mercifully dealt with; but they are taken quite seriously for all that. [Draft ends here]

The Pickwick Pantomime

Unsigned review of a reprint of the first edition of *The Posthumous Papers of the Pickwick Club*, with an introduction by Charles Dickens the Younger. *Daily Chronicle* (London), 14 April 1892.

The most curious passage in this reprint occurs in a letter which Dickens wrote in 1866, twenty-nine years after the publication of *Pickwick*, asking his son to obtain Mrs. Dickens's written testimony to the fact that Seymour, the artist[1], had nothing to do with the invention of the book. The last paragraph runs thus:

> It seems a superfluous precaution, but I take it for the sake of our descendants long after you.

These words leave no reasonable doubt that the *Pickwick Papers*, in Dickens's maturest judgment, were good enough to be described, in the current literary slang, as "immortal." And certainly there is no denying that when a book which was unprecedentedly popular half a century ago is at present more popular than ever it is waste of time to argue against its claim to rank as an English classic. But there are pages upon pages of *Pickwick* which explain the coldness with which it was received by literary experts at first, which make you lay the book down, and say to yourself: "Supposing I had not been a child when this first fell into my hands—supposing I had been an educated critic, and had formed my taste upon *Jonathan Wild* and *A Tale of a Tub*, in which the Pickwickian literary style is to be found in the full strength of its original purity and artistic integrity, would I not have been revolted by Dickens's conscious and insistent facetiousness, by his lapses into journalistic carelessness and commonplace, by the melodramatic vulgarity of his tragic episodes? Would it not have seemed an inept, juvenile, unappreciative imitation—an adulteration, in short—of Swift and Fielding?" Then comes the still more puzzling question, How long would that critical attitude have lasted? Macaulay, as we know, gave in when

---

[1]Robert Seymour (1800?–36), English illustrator, had provided only seven plates for *Pickwick Papers* when he committed suicide. Dickens had been commissioned originally to write for the illustrations.

he came to Jingle's anecdotes on the Rochester coach, having held
out for only twelve pages—just up to the point at which it becomes
apparent that whatever the author's style may be he is working a
mine of whimsical invention which no writer could possess and be
poor in the essential qualities of a humourist. A deeper critic would
probably have succumbed sooner rather than later. We fail to
appreciate the power of observation displayed in the opening chapter, with its report of the meeting of the Pickwick Club, not at all
because it is barefaced and overdone, but because either we have
not seen as much of learned societies' meetings as Dickens did in his
early reporting days, or else we have been more successfully
imposed upon than he by the seriousness with which such bodies
take themselves.

The general public, all innocence and reverent faith in public
institutions, can never, indeed, be persuaded that Dickens was not a
caricaturist. He has never been reproached with cynicism: all his
ridiculous pictures of political and academic life pass as jocose
exaggerations; and the real secret of the pre-eminence of *Pickwick*
in point of popularity over all his other books is that it is the only
one which can be read without an occasional uncomfortable suspicion that the author was in downright earnest after all. When he
wrote it he had observed accurately enough, but he had not taken
to heart what he had observed. His view of politics in it is often that
of a rowdy undergraduate; and it is not too much to say that his
view of humanity is sometimes that of a street arab. The Eatanswill
election, though it is a faithful picture of what a country election
would be to-day if the Corrupt Practices Act and Vote by Ballot
were abolished, is described in all possible lightness of heart as a
rare lark; whilst as to the characters, although they, too, are bit off
accurately enough, he does nothing in chapter after chapter but
laugh at Tupman for being fat, at the spinster aunt for being an old
maid, at Tony Weller for being an apoplectic coachman, and at
Winkle for being a duffer; whilst Jingle, Job [Trotter], Sam Weller
and the Fat Boy form a harlequinade pure and simple, in which Mr.
Pickwick himself, in spite of the affection which Dickens conceived
for him as he warmed to his work, and as success encouraged him
to take himself seriously, figures as the king of pantaloons. Our
love and esteem for the "angel in tights and gaiters" must not blind

us to the fact that Mr. Pickwick repeatedly gets drunk, and is tumbled head over heels, knocked about with fire-shovels and carpet bags, cuffed, cheated, mulcted, duped, haled before the magistrate, put in the pound, and pelted with turnips and rotten eggs, not to mention his mistaking a lady's bed for his own and getting into serious trouble in consequence. But it must be confessed that the Pickwickian harlequinade, as a harlequinade, is incomparable. As Gounod said of *Don Giovanni*, it is a summit in art beyond which no man can go without precipitous descent to the Albert Smith level[2]. The old women in it, Mrs. Cluppins, Mrs. Sanders, Mrs. Bardell, Mrs. Weller, and the incomparable Mrs. Raddle, though they are treated with remorseless inhumanity, are none the less horribly and squalidly funny. Grummer, with his six special constables, eclipses all the stage policemen that Drury Lane has ever seen. In fact the whole entertainment is raised by its very intensity to the keenness of high comedy, and the glow and vigour of melodrama. Jingle, impossible as he is, seems almost like the truth about Mercadet and Robert Macaire; and Sam Weller has more of Sganarelle than of Joey in him[3]. Indeed, Molière might have written a *Pickwick* had he been let run wild from all artistic tradition and provided with a British middle-class audience. The only figure of the conventional harlequinade which Dickens left as he found it—and the failure is significant of his cardinal disability as a novelist—is the columbine. There are several attempts at her— Arabella Allen, the pretty housemaid, Emily Wardle, &c.; but each seems the most hopeless doll in the set until we turn to the other and pronounce her worse. Still, who cares about the columbine being a doll when she has such a brother as Ben Allen and such an unsuccessful wooer as Bob Sawyer?

Later on, when Dickens realised that the people who so tickled his sense of the ridiculous were human beings like himself, and that

[2]Albert R. Smith (1816–60), a humorous writer, was one of the earliest contributors to *Punch*.

[3]Mercadet is a speculator in Balzac's comedy *Le Faiseur* (1830), later produced successfully as a drama, *Mercadet* (1840), in an adaptation by Adolphe Philippe d'Ennery. Robert Macaire, subject of a play by Robert Louis Stevenson and W. E. Henley (1892), first appeared as the villain of a melodrama, *L'Auberge des Adrets* (1823), by Benjamin Antiers, Saint-Amand, and Paulyanthe. Sganarelle, in this context, refers to the pusillanimous servant in Molière's *Dom Juan* (1665).

the merry Eatanswill game was being played not for fun, but for solid plunder, the cost of which in human life and happiness no man could calculate, his humour came to be much less appreciated than before. For example, no figure in the *Pickwick* collection is funnier than the fatuous Mr. Sparkler in *Little Dorrit*; and the conferring of a public appointment on Mr. Sparkler is at the same time more farcical and more deeply observed and scrupulously and knowledgeably described than the return of the Honourable Samuel Slumkey as the "representative" in Parliament of the unsoaped of Eatanswill. But in *Little Dorrit* the jobbery of Mr. Sparkler's sinecure, however sardonically laughable its details may be, leaves the reader much more uneasy than the death of the Chancery prisoner in the Fleet Prison in *Pickwick*. Again, in *Great Expectations*, the transactions of the club of rich young men called "The Finches of the Grove" are far more ludicrous and more convincing than the debate on Mr. Pickwick's theory of tittlebats, or his learned interpretation of BILST UM PHSHI S.M. ARK; but they form part of a tragedy for all that—the tragedy of the miserable emptiness and shiftlessness of the life which society offers to such young men; and you laugh with the wrong side of your mouth.

After all, one can quite understand how it was that though *Little Dorrit* and *Great Expectations* are immeasurably the greatest works of their kind which the century has produced in England, *Pickwick* being mere schoolboy tomfoolery in comparison, yet the public cling to *Pickwick*, and there is quite a school of critics who feel that Dickens took an essentially ungentlemanly view of things, and try to believe that poor Thackeray, though a shocking cynic, was much the deeper of the two. The thought of setting up Thackeray against a novelist so prodigiously and obviously his superior as Dickens must have been fathered by a very bitter wish. It shows how very hard Dickens succeeded in hitting the conscience of Society after that remarkable shattering of his complacent domestic ideals, and awakening to the broader social issues, which were marked in his career by the break up of his family life and the writing of *Hard Times*. No wonder we fly from our consciences to the careless humours of Nupkins and the homely but pungent satires of the long gamekeeper [in Chapter 19] upon Mr. Winkle's shooting. And it may well be that long after those terrible cases of conscience which are thrust on us in *Great Expectations* and *Little Dorrit* have been settled and happily forgotten, we shall still enjoy our thoughtless heehaw over *Pickwick*, which may consequently survive the other two, not as the greatest, but as the fittest. Let us hope so, at any rate.

It is only necessary to say concerning this new edition of the *Pickwick Papers* that it is the latest number of Messrs. Macmillan's 3s. 6d. series of works by popular authors; that all the old illustrations by Seymour and Phiz,[4] with the design for the wrapper of the original monthly parts, have been reproduced, presumably by photographic process, from a set of good impressions from the plates, and that an introduction has been contributed by Mr. Charles Dickens [the Younger], whose conduct will, perhaps, strike Messrs. Chapman and Hall, the holders of the recently-expired copyright, as "wery far from fillal."

---

[4]"Phiz" was the pseudonym of Hablôt Knight Browne (1815–82), who provided illustrations for all of Dickens's novels through *A Tale of Two Cities* (1859).

Introduction to *Hard Times*

Written for the Waverley (London) subscription edition (1913).

John Ruskin once declared *Hard Times* Dickens's best novel. It is worth while asking why Ruskin thought this, because he would have been the first to admit that the habit of placing works of art in competition with one another, and wrangling as to which is the best, is the habit of the sportsman, not of the enlightened judge of art. Let us take it that what Ruskin meant was that *Hard Times* was one of his special favorites among Dickens's books. Was this the caprice of fancy? or is there any rational explanation of the preference? I think there is.

Hard Times is the first fruit of that very interesting occurrence which our religious sects call, sometimes conversion, sometimes being saved, sometimes attaining to conviction of sin. Now the great conversions of the XIX century were not convictions of individual, but of social sin. The first half of the XIX century considered itself the greatest of all the centuries. The second discovered that it was the wickedest of all the centuries. The first half despised and pitied the Middle Ages as barbarous, cruel, superstitious, ignorant. The second half saw no hope for mankind except in the recovery of the faith, the art, the humanity of the Middle Ages. In Macaulay's *History of England*, the world is so happy, so progressive, so firmly set in the right path, that the author cannot mention even the National Debt without proclaiming that the deeper the country goes into debt, the more it prospers. In Morris's *News from Nowhere* there is nothing left of all the institutions that Macaulay glorified except an old building, so ugly that it is used only as a manure market, that was once the British House of Parliament. *Hard Times* was written in 1854, just at the turn of the half century; and in it we see Dickens with his eyes newly open and his conscience newly stricken by the discovery of the real state of England. In the book that went immediately before, *Bleak House*, he was still denouncing evils and ridiculing absurdities that were mere symptoms of the anarchy that followed the industrial revolution of the XVIII and XIX centuries, and the conquest of political power by Commercialism in 1832. In *Bleak House* Dickens knows nothing of the industrial revolution: he imagines that what is wrong is that when a dispute arises over the division of the plunder of the nation, the Court of Chancery, instead of settling the dispute cheaply and promptly, beggars the disputants and pockets both their shares. His description of our party system, with its Coodle, Doodle, Foodle, etc., has never been surpassed for accuracy and for penetration of superficial pretence. But he had not dug down to the bed rock of the imposture. His portrait of the ironmaster who visits Sir Leicester Dedlock, and who is so solidly superior to him, might have been drawn by Macaulay: there is not a touch of Bounderby in it. His horrible and not untruthful portraits of the brickmakers whose abject and battered wives call them "master," and his picture of the now vanished slum between Drury Lane and Catherine Street which he calls Tom All Alone's, suggest (save in the one case of the outcast Jo, who is, like Oliver Twist, a child, and therefore outside the old self-help panacea of Dickens's time) nothing but individual delinquencies, local plague-spots, negligent authorities.

In *Hard Times* you will find all this changed. Coketown, which you can see to-day for yourself in all its grime in the Potteries (the real name of it is Hanley in Staffordshire on the London and North Western Railway), is not, like Tom All Alone's, a patch of slum in a fine city, easily cleared away, as Tom's actually was about fifty years after Dickens called attention to it. Coketown is the whole place; and its rich manufacturers are proud of its dirt, and declare that they like to see the sun blacked out with smoke, because it means that the furnaces are busy and money is being made; whilst its poor factory hands have never known any other sort of town, and are as content with it as a rat is with a hole. Mr. Rouncewell, the pillar of society who snubs Sir Leicester with such dignity, has become Mr. Bounderby, the self-made humbug. The Chancery suitors who are driving themselves mad by hanging about the Courts in the hope of getting a judgment in their favor instead of trying to earn an honest living, are replaced by factory operatives who toil miserably and incessantly only to see the streams of gold they set flowing slip through their fingers into the pockets of men who revile and oppress them.

Clearly this is not the Dickens who burlesqued the old song of the "Fine Old English Gentleman,"[1] and saw in the evils he attacked only the sins and wickednesses and follies of a great civilization. This is Karl Marx, Carlyle, Ruskin, Morris, Carpenter, rising up against civilization itself as against a disease, and declaring that it is not our disorder but our order that is horrible; that it is not our criminals but our magnates that are robbing and murdering us; and that it is not merely Tom All Alone's that must be demolished and abolished, pulled down, rooted up, and made for ever impossible so that nothing shall remain of it but History's record of its infamy, but our entire social system. For that was how men felt, and how some of them spoke, in the early days of the Great Conversion which produced, first, such books as the Latter Day Pamphlets of Carlyle, Dickens's *Hard Times*, and the tracts and sociological novels of the Christian Socialists, and later on the Socialist movement which has now spread all over the world, and which has succeeded in convincing even those who most abhor the name of Socialism that the condition of the civilized world is deplorable, and that the remedy is far beyond the means of individual righteousness. In short, whereas formerly men said to the victim of society who ventured to complain, "Go and reform yourself before you pretend to reform Society," it now has to admit that until Society is reformed, no man can reform himself except in the most insignificantly small ways. He may cease picking your pocket of half crowns; but he cannot cease taking a quarter of a million a year from the community for nothing at one end of the scale, or living under conditions in which health, decency, and gentleness are impossible at the other, if he happens to be born to such a lot.

You must therefore resign yourself, if you are reading Dickens's books in the order in which they were written, to bid adieu now to the light-hearted and only occasionally indignant Dickens of the earlier books, and get such entertainment as you can from him now that the occasional indignation has spread and deepened into a passionate revolt against the whole industrial order of the modern world. Here you will find no more villains and heroes, but only oppressors and victims, oppressing and suffering in spite of them-

[1]Dickens's "The Fine Old English Gentleman: New Version (To be said or sung at all Conservative Dinners)," an anti-Tory rhymed lampoon, was published in *The Examiner* (London) on 7 August 1841, signed "W."

selves, driven by a huge machinery which grinds to pieces the people it should nourish and ennoble, and having for its directors the basest and most foolish of us instead of the noblest and most farsighted.

Many readers find the change disappointing. Others find Dickens worth reading almost for the first time. The increase in strength and intensity is enormous: the power that indicts a nation so terribly is much more impressive than that which ridicules individuals. But it cannot be said that there is an increase of simple pleasure for the reader, though the books are not therefore less attractive. One cannot say that it is pleasanter to look at a battle than at a merry-go-round; but there can be no question which draws the larger crowd.

To describe the change in the readers' feelings more precisely, one may say that it is impossible to enjoy Gradgrind or Bounderby as one enjoys Pecksniff or the Artful Dodger or Mrs. Gamp or Micawber or Dick Swiveller, because these earlier characters have nothing to do with us except to amuse us. We neither hate nor fear them. We do not expect ever to meet them, and should not be in the least afraid of them if we did. England is not full of Micawbers and Swivellers. They are not our fathers, our schoolmasters, our employers, our tyrants. We do not read novels to escape from them and forget them: quite the contrary. But England is full of Bounderbys and Podsnaps and Gradgrinds; and we are all to a quite appalling extent in their power. We either hate and fear them or else we *are* them, and resent being held up to odium by a novelist. We have only to turn to the article on Dickens in the current edition of the *Encyclopedia Britannica* to find how desperately our able critics still exalt all Dickens's early stories about individuals whilst ignoring or belittling such masterpieces as *Hard Times*, *Little Dorrit*, *Our Mutual Friend*, and even *Bleak House* (because of Sir Leicester Dedlock), for their mercilessly faithful and penetrating exposures of English social, industrial, and political life; to see how hard Dickens hits the conscience of the governing class; and how loth we still are to confess, not that we are so wicked (for of that we are rather proud), but so ridiculous, so futile, so incapable of making our country really prosperous. *The Old Curiosity Shop* was written to amuse you, entertain you, touch you; and it succeeded.

Hard Times was written to make you uncomfortable; and it will make you uncomfortable (and serve you right) though it will perhaps interest you more, and certainly leave a deeper scar on you, than any two of its forerunners.

At the same time you need not fear to find Dickens losing his good humor and sense of fun and becoming serious in Mr. Gradgrind's way. On the contrary, Dickens in this book casts off, and casts off for ever, all restraint on his wild sense of humor. He had always been inclined to break loose: there are passages in the speeches of Mrs. Nickleby and Pecksniff which are impossible as well as funny. But now it is no longer a question of passages: here he begins at last to exercise quite recklessly his power of presenting a character to you in the most fantastic and outrageous terms, putting into its mouth from one end of the book to the other hardly one word which could conceivably be uttered by any sane human being, and yet leaving you with an unmistakeable and exactly truthful portrait of a character that you recognize at once as not only real but typical. Nobody ever talked, or ever will talk, as Silas Wegg talks to Boffin and Mr. Venus, or as Mr. Venus reports Pleasant Riderhood to have talked, or as Rogue Riderhood talks, or as John Chivery talks. They utter rhapsodies of nonsense conceived in an ecstasy of mirth. And this begins in *Hard Times*. Jack Bunsby in *Dombey and Son* is absurd: the oracles he delivers are very nearly impossible, and yet not quite impossible. But Mrs. Sparsit in this book, though Rembrandt could not have drawn a certain type of real woman more precisely to the life, is grotesque from beginning to end in her way of expressing herself. Her nature, her tricks of manner, her way of taking Mr. Bounderby's marriage, her instinct for hunting down Louisa and Mrs. Pegler, are drawn with an unerring hand; and she says nothing that is out of character. But no clown gone suddenly mad in a very mad harlequinade could express all these truths in more extravagantly ridiculous speeches. Dickens's business in life has become too serious for troubling over the small change of verisimilitude, and denying himself and his readers the indulgence of his humor in inessentials. He even calls the schoolmaster McChoakumchild, which is almost an insult to the serious reader. And it was so afterwards to the end of his life. There are moments when he imperils the whole effect of his character drawing by some overpoweringly comic sally. For instance, happening in *Hard Times* to describe Mr. Bounderby as drumming on his hat as if it were a tambourine, which is quite correct and natural, he presently says that "Mr. Bounderby put his tambourine on his head, like an oriental dancer." Which similitude is so unexpectedly and excruciatingly funny that it is almost impossible to feel duly angry with the odious Bounderby afterwards.

This disregard of naturalness in speech is extraordinarily entertaining in the comic method; but it must be admitted that it is not only not entertaining, but sometimes hardly bearable when it does not make us laugh. There are two persons in *Hard Times*, Louisa Gradgrind and Cissy Jupe, who are serious throughout. Louisa is a figure of poetic tragedy; and there is no question of naturalness in her case: she speaks from beginning to end as an inspired prophetess, conscious of her own doom and finally bearing to her father the judgment of Providence on his blind conceit. If you once consent to overlook her marriage, which is none the less an act of prostitution because she does it to obtain advantages for her brother and not for herself, there is nothing in the solemn poetry of her deadly speech that jars. But Cissy is nothing if not natural; and though Cissy is as true to nature in her character as Mrs. Sparsit, she "speaks like a book" in the most intolerable sense of the words. In her interview with Mr. James Harthouse, her unconscious courage and simplicity, and his hopeless defeat by them, are quite natural and right; and the contrast between the humble girl of the people and the smart sarcastic man of the world whom she so completely vanquishes is excellently dramatic; but Dickens has allowed himself to be carried away by the scene into a ridiculous substitution of his own most literary and least colloquial style for any language that could conceivably be credited to Cissy.

"Mr. Harthouse: the only reparation that remains with you is to leave her immediately and finally. I am quite sure that you can mitigate in no other way the wrong and harm you have done. I am quite sure that it is the only compensation you have left it in your power to make. I do not say that it is much, or that it is enough; but it is something, and it is necessary. Therefore, though without any other authority than I have given you, and even without the knowledge of any other person than yourself and myself, I ask you to depart from this place to-night, under an obligation never to return to it."

This is the language of a Lord Chief Justice, not of the dunce of an elementary school in the Potteries.

But this is only a surface failure, just as the extravagances of Mrs. Sparsit are only surface extravagances. There is, however, one real failure in the book. Slackbridge, the trade union organizer, is a mere figment of the middle-class imagination. No such man would be listened to by a meeting of English factory hands. Not that such meetings are less susceptible to humbug than meetings of any other class. Not that trade union organizers, worn out by the terribly wearisome and trying work of going from place to place repeating the same commonplaces and trying to "stoke up" meetings to enthusiasm with them, are less apt than other politicians to end as windbags, and sometimes to depend on stimulants to pull them through their work. Not, in short, that the trade union platform is any less humbug-ridden than the platforms of our more highly placed political parties. But even at their worst trade union organiz- ers are not a bit like Slackbridge. Note, too, that Dickens mentions that there was a chairman at the meeting (as if that were rather surprising), and that this chairman makes no attempt to preserve the usual order of public meeting, but allows speakers to address the assembly and interrupt one another in an entirely disorderly way. All this is pure middle-class ignorance. It is much as if a tramp were to write a description of millionaires smoking large cigars in church, with their wives in low-necked dresses and diamonds. We cannot say that Dickens did not know the working classes, because he knew humanity too well to be ignorant of any class. But this sort of knowledge is as compatible with ignorance of class manners and customs as with ignorance of foreign languages. Dickens knew certain classes of working folk very well: domestic servants, village artisans, and employees of petty tradesmen, for example. But of the segregated factory populations of our purely industrial towns he knew no more than an observant professional man can pick up on a flying visit to Manchester.

It is especially important to notice that Dickens expressly says in this book that the workers were wrong to organize themselves in trade unions, thereby endorsing what was perhaps the only practical mistake of the Gradgrind school that really mattered much. And having thus thoughtlessly adopted, or at least repeated, this error, long since exploded, of the philosophic Radical school from which he started, he turns his back frankly on Democracy, and adopts the idealized Toryism of Carlyle and Ruskin, in which the aristocracy are the masters and superiors of the people, and also the servants of the people and of God. Here is a significant passage.

"Now perhaps," said Mr. Bounderby, "you will let the gentleman know how you would set this muddle (as you are so fond of calling it) to rights."

"I donno, sir. I canna be expecten to't. Tis not me as should be looken to for that, sir. Tis they as is put ower me, and ower aw the rest of us. What do they tak upon themseln, sir, if not to do it?"

And to this Dickens sticks for the rest of his life. In *Our Mutual Friend* he appeals again and again to the governing classes, asking them with every device of reproach, invective, sarcasm, and ridicule of which he is master, what they have to say to this or that evil which it is their professed business to amend or avoid. Nowhere does he appeal to the working classes to take their fate into their own hands and try the democratic plan.

Another phrase used by Stephen Blackpool in this remarkable fifth chapter is important. "Nor yet lettin alone will never do it." It is Dickens's express repudiation of *laissez-faire*.

There is nothing more in the book that needs any glossary, except, perhaps, the strange figure of the Victorian "swell," Mr. James Harthouse. His pose has gone out of fashion. Here and there you may still see a man—even a youth—with a single eyeglass, an elaborately bored and weary air, and a little stock of cynicisms and indifferentisms contrasting oddly with a mortal anxiety about his clothes. All he needs is a pair of Dundreary whiskers,[2] like the officers in Desanges' military pictures,[3] to be a fair imitation of Mr. James Harthouse. But he is not in the fashion: he is an eccentric, as Whistler was an eccentric, as Max Beerbohm and the neo-dandies

[2]Lord Dundreary is the title character in Tom Taylor's comedy *Our American Cousin* (1858). The stage makeup, affected by the original performer, consisting of silky whiskers divided to form two long points, set a new fashion in London.
[3]Louis-William Desanges (1822–?), English-born French artist, was noted for paintings on military subjects and equestrian portraits.

of the *fin de siècle* were eccentrics. It is now the fashion to be strenuous, to be energetic, to hustle as American millionaires are supposed (rather erroneously) to hustle. But the soul of the swell is still unchanged. He has changed his name again and again, become a Masher, a Toff, a Johnny and what not; but fundamentally he remains what he always was, an Idler, and therefore a man bound to find some trick of thought and speech that reduces the world to a thing as empty and purposeless and hopeless as himself. Mr. Harthouse reappears, more seriously and kindly taken, as Eugene Wrayburn and Mortimer Lightwood in *Our Mutual Friend*. He reappears as a club in The Finches of the Grove in *Great Expectations*. He will reappear in all his essentials in fact and in fiction until he is at last shamed or coerced into honest industry and becomes not only unintelligible but inconceivable.

Note, finally, that in this book Dickens proclaims that marriages are not made in heaven, and that those which are not confirmed there, should be dissolved.

What is the New Element in the Norwegian School?

A chapter written in 1913 for an expanded second edition of *The Quintessence of Ibsenism* (first published in 1891).

I now come to the question: Why, since neither human nature nor the specific talent of the playwright has changed since the days of Charles Dickens and Dumas *père*, are the works of Ibsen, of Strindberg, of Tolstoy, of Gorki, of Tchekov, of Brieux[1], so different from those of the great fictionists of the first half of the nineteenth century? Tolstoy actually imitated Dickens. Ibsen was not Dickens's superior as an observer, nor is Strindberg, nor Gorki, nor Tchekov, nor Brieux. Tolstoy and Ibsen together, gifted as they were, were not otherwise gifted or more gifted than Shakespear and Molière. Yet a generation which could read all Shakespear and Molière, Dickens and Dumas, from end to end without the smallest intellectual or ethical perturbation, was unable to get through a play by Ibsen or a novel by Tolstoy without having its intellectual and moral complacency upset, its religious faith shattered, and its notions of right and wrong conduct thrown into confusion and sometimes even reversed. It is as if these modern men had a spiritual force that was lacking in even the greatest of their forerunners. And yet, what evidence is there in the lives of Wagner, Ibsen, Tolstoy, Strindberg, Gorki, Tchekov, and Brieux, that they were or are better men in any sense than Shakespear, Molière, Dickens, and Dumas?

I myself have been told by people that the reading of a single book of mine or the witnessing of a single play has changed their whole lives; and among these are some who tell me that they cannot read Dickens at all, whilst all of them have read books and seen plays by authors obviously quite as gifted as I am, without finding anything more in them than pastime.

The explanation is to be found in what I believe to be a general law of the evolution of ideas. "Every jest is an earnest in the womb of time" says Peter Keegan in *John Bull's Other Island*. "There's many a true word spoken in jest" says the first villager you engage in philosophic discussion. All very serious revolutionary proposi-

[1] Eugène Brieux (1858–1932), French dramatist and social critic, whose work was vastly overrated by Shaw in a preface to *Three Plays by Brieux* (1911).

tions begin as huge jokes. Otherwise they would be stamped out by the lynching of their first exponents. Even these exponents themselves have their revelations broken to them mysteriously through their sense of humor. Two friends of mine, travelling in remote parts of Spain, were asked by the shepherds what their religion was. "Our religion," replied one of them, a very highly cultivated author and traveller, with a sardonic turn, "is that there is no God." This reckless remark, taken seriously, might have provided nineteenth century scepticism with a martyr. As it was, the countryside rang with laughter for days afterwards as the stupendous joke was handed round. But it was just by tolerating the blasphemy as a joke that the shepherds began to build it into the fabric of their minds. Being now safely lodged there, it will in due time develop its earnestness; and at last travellers will come who will be taken quite seriously when they say that the imaginary hidalgo in the sky whom the shepherds call God does indeed not exist. And they will remain godless, and call their streets Avenue Paul Bert[2] and so forth, until in due time another joker will arrive with sidesplitting intimations that Shakespear's "There's a divinity that shapes our ends, rough hew them how we will"[3] was a strictly scientific statement of fact, and that "neo-Darwinism" consists for the most part of grossly unscientific statements of superstitious nonsense. Which jest will in its due time come to its own as very solid earnest.

The same phenomenon may be noticed in our attitude towards matters of fact so obvious that no dispute can arise as to their existence. And here the power of laughter is astonishing. It is not enough to say merely that men enable themselves to endure the unbearablest nuisances and the deadliest scourges by setting up a merry convention that they are amusing. We must go further and face the fact that they actually are amused by them—that they are not laughing with the wrong side of the mouth. If you doubt it, read the popular fiction of the pre-Dickensian age, from the novels of Smollett to *Tom Cringle's Log*.[4] Poverty in rags is a joke, yellow fever is a joke, drunkenness is a joke, dysentery is a joke, kickings, floggings, falls, frights, humiliations, and painful accidents of all

[2]Paul Bert (1833–86), French physiologist and politician, notoriously anticlerical.
[3]*Hamlet*, V.ii.10.
[4]Michael Scott's *Tom Cringle's Log* (1833) is a novel of nautical adventure.

sorts are jokes. Henpecked husbands and termagant mothers-in-law are prime jokes. The infirmities of age and the inexperience and shyness of youth are jokes; and it is first-rate fun to insult and torment those that suffer from them.

We take some of these jokes seriously enough now. *Humphrey Clinker* may not have become absolutely unreadable (I have not tried him for more than forty years); but there is certainly a good deal in the book that is now simply disgusting to the class of reader that in its own day found it uproariously amusing. Much of *Tom Cringle* has become mere savagery: its humors are those of a donkey race. Also, the fun is forced: one sees beneath the determination of the old sea dog to put a hearty smiling English face on pain and discomfort, that he has not merely looked on at it, and that he did not really like it. The mask of laughter wears slowly off the shames and the evils; but men finally see them as they really are.

Sometimes the change occurs, not between two generations, but actually in the course of a single work by one author. Don Quixote and Mr. Pickwick are recognized examples of characters introduced in pure ridicule, and presently gaining the affection and finally the respect of their authors. To them may be added Shakespear's Falstaff. Falstaff is introduced as a subordinate stage figure with no other function than to be robbed by the Prince and Poins, who was originally meant to be the *raisonneur* of the piece, and the chief figure among the prince's dissolute associates. But Poins soon fades into nothing, like several characters in Dickens's early works; whilst Falstaff develops into an enormous joke and an exquisitely mimicked human type. Only in the end the joke withers. The question comes to Shakespear: *Is* this really a laughing matter? Of course there can be only one answer; and Shakespear gives it as best he can by the mouth of the prince become king, who might, one thinks, have the decency to wait until he has redeemed his own character before assuming the right to lecture his boon companion. Falstaff, rebuked and humiliated, dies miserably. His followers are hanged, except Pistol, whose exclamation "Old do I wax; and from my weary limbs honor is cudgelled"[5] is a melancholy exordium to an old age of beggary and imposture.

[5]*Henry V*, V.i.89.

But suppose Shakespear had begun where he left off! Suppose he had been born at a time when, as the result of a long propaganda of health and temperance, sack had come to be called alcohol, alcohol had come to be called poison, corpulence had come to be regarded as either a disease or a breach of good manners, and a conviction had spread throughout society that the practice of consuming "a half-pennyworth of bread to an intolerable deal of sack"[6] was the cause of so much misery, crime, and racial degeneration that whole States prohibited the sale of potable spirits altogether, and even moderate drinking was more and more regarded as a regrettable weakness! Suppose (to drive the change well home) the women in the great theatrical centres had completely lost that amused indulgence for the drunken man which still exists in some out-of-the-way places, and felt nothing but disgust and anger at the conduct and habits of Falstaff and Sir Toby Belch! Instead of *Henry IV* and *The Merry Wives of Windsor*, we should have had something like Zola's *L'Assommoir*. Indeed, we actually have Cassio, the last of Shakespear's gentleman-drunkards, talking like a temperance reformer, a fact which suggests that Shakespear had been roundly lectured for the offensive vulgarity of Sir Toby by some woman of refinement who refused to see the smallest fun in giving a knight such a name as Belch, with characteristics to correspond to it. Suppose, again, that the first performance of *The Taming of the Shrew* had led to a modern Feminist demonstration in the theatre, and forced upon Shakespear's consideration a whole century of agitatresses, from Mary Wollstonecraft to Mrs. Fawcett and Mrs. Pankhurst,[7] is it not likely that the jest of Katharine and Petruchio would have become the earnest of Nora and Torvald Helmer?

In this light the difference between Dickens and Strindberg becomes intelligible. Strindberg simply refuses to regard the cases of Mrs. Raddle and Mrs. MacStinger and Mrs. Joe Gargery as laughing matters. He insists on taking them seriously as cases of a tyranny which effects more degradation and causes more misery

[6]*Henry IV, Part II*, II.iv.591–92.
[7]Mary Wollstonecraft (Godwin) (1759–97) an early feminist, wrote *Vindication of the Rights of Women* (1792). Millicent Garrett Fawcett (1847–1929) and Emmeline Pankhurst (1858–1928) were leaders in the English suffragist movement a century later.

than all the political and sectarian oppressions known to history. Yet it cannot be said that Strindberg, even at his fiercest, is harder on women than Dickens. No doubt his case against them is far more complete, because he does not shirk the specifically sexual factors in it. But this really softens it. If Dickens had allowed us, were it but for an instant, to see Joe Gargery and Mrs. Joe as husband and wife, he would perhaps have been accused by fools of immodesty; but we should have at least some more human impression than the one left by an unredeemed shrew married to a grown-up terrified child. It was George Gissing, a modern realist, who first pointed out the power and truth to nature of Dickens's women, and the fact that, funny as they are, they are mostly detestable.[8] Even the amiable ones are silly and sometimes disastrous. When the few good ones are agreeable they are not specifically feminine: they are the Dickensian good man in petticoats; yet they lack that strength which they would have had if Dickens had seen clearly that there is no such species in creation as "Woman, lovely woman,"[9] the woman being simply the female of the human species, and that to have one conception of humanity for the woman and another for the man, or one law for the woman and another for the man, or one artistic convention for woman and another for man or, for the matter of that, a skirt for the woman and a pair of breeches for the man, is as unnatural, and in the long run as unworkable, as one law for the mare and another for the horse. Roughly it may be said that all Dickens's studies from life of the differentiated creatures our artificial sex institutions have made of women are, for all their truth, either vile or ridiculous or both. Betsey Trotwood is a dear because she is an old bachelor in petticoats: a manly woman, like all good women: good men being equally all womanly men. Miss Havisham, an insanely womanly woman, is a horror, a monster, though a Chinese monster: that is, not a natural one, but one produced by deliberate perversion of her humanity. In comparison, Strindberg's women are positively amiable and attractive. The general impression that Strindberg's women are the revenge of a furious woman-hater for his domestic failures, whilst Dickens is a

[8]*Charles Dickens: A Critical Study* (1898).
[9]Thomas Otway, *Venice Preserv'd* (1682).

genial idealist (he had little better luck domestically, by the way), is produced solely by Dickens either making fun of the affair or believing that women are born so and must be admitted to the fellowship of the Holy Ghost on a feminine instead of a human basis; whilst Strindberg takes womanliness with deadly seriousness as an evil not to be submitted to for a moment without vehement protest and demand for quite practicable reform. The nurse in his play who wheedles her old nursling and then slips a strait waistcoat on him revolts us; but she is really ten times more lovable and sympathetic than Sairey Gamp, an abominable creature whose very soul is putrid, and who is yet true to life. It is very noteworthy that none of the modern writers who take life as seriously as Ibsen have ever been able to bring themselves to depict depraved people so pitilessly as Dickens and Thackeray and even the genial Dumas *père*. Ibsen was grim enough in all conscience: no man has said more terrible things both privately and publicly; and yet there is not one of Ibsen's characters who is not, in the old phrase, the temple of the Holy Ghost,[10] and who does not move you at moments by the sense of that mystery. The Dickens-Thackeray spirit is, in comparison, that of a Punch and Judy showman, who is never restrained from whacking his little figures unmercifully by the sense that they, too, are images of God, and, "but for the grace of God," very like himself. Dickens does deepen very markedly towards this as he grows older, though it is impossible to pretend that Mrs. Wilfer is treated with less levity than Mrs. Nickleby; but to Ibsen, from beginning to end, every human being is a sacrifice, whilst to Dickens he is a farce. And there you have the whole difference. No character drawn by Dickens is more ridiculous than Hjalmar Ekdal in *The Wild Duck*, or more eccentric than old Ekdal, whose toy game-preserve in the garret is more fantastic than the house of Miss Havisham; and yet these Ekdals wring the heart whilst Micawber and Chivery (who sits between the lines of clothes hung out to dry because "it reminds him of groves" as Hjalmar's garret reminds old Ekdal of bear forests) only shake the sides.

It may be that if Dickens could read these lines he would say that the defect was not in him but in his readers; and that if we will return to his books now that Ibsen has opened our eyes we will have to admit that he also saw more in the soul of Micawber than mere laughing gas. And indeed one cannot forget the touches of kindliness and gallantry which ennoble his mirth. Still, between the man who occasionally remembered and the man who never forgot, between Dick Swiveller and Ulrik Brendel,[11] there is a mighty difference. The most that can be said to minimize it is that some of the difference is certainly due to the difference in the attitude of the reader. When an author's works produce violent controversy, and are new, people are apt to read them with that sort of seriousness which is very appropriately called deadly: that is, with a sort of solemn paralysis of every sense except a quite abstract and baseless momentousness which has no more to do with the contents of the author's works than the horrors of a man in delirium tremens have to do with real rats and snakes. The Bible is a sealed literature to most of us because we cannot read it naturally and unsophisticatedly: we are like the old lady who was edified by the word Mesopotamia, or Samuel Butler's Chowbok,[12] who was converted to Christianity by the effect on his imagination of the prayer for Queen Adelaide. Many years elapsed before those who were impressed with Beethoven's music ventured to enjoy it sufficiently to discover what a large part of it is a riot of whimsical fun. As to Ibsen, I remember a performance of *The Wild Duck*, at which the late Clement Scott pointed out triumphantly that the play was so absurd that even the champions of Ibsen could not help laughing at it.[13] It had not occurred to him that Ibsen could laugh like other men. Not until an author has become so familiar that we are quite at our ease with him, and are up to his tricks of manner, do we cease to imagine that he is, relatively to older writers, terribly serious.

Still, the utmost allowance we can make for this difference does not persuade us that Dickens took the improvidence and futility of Micawber as Ibsen took the improvidence and futility of Hjalmar

---

[11]A character in Ibsen's *Rosmersholm* (1886).
[12]A character in Butler's *Erewhon* (1872).
[13]Clement Scott (1841–1904), drama critic of the *Daily Telegraph* (London) had stated in an unsigned notice on 5 May 1894 that Ekdal in *The Wild Duck* was unable to decide whether "he should represent a mild Micawber or an attenuated Harold Skimpole."

Ekdal. The difference is plain in the works of Dickens himself; for the Dickens of the second half of the nineteenth century (the Ibsen half) is a different man from the Dickens of the first half. From *Hard Times* and *Little Dorrit* to *Our Mutual Friend* every one of Dickens's books lays a heavy burden on our conscience without flattering us with any hopes of a happy ending. But from *The Pickwick Papers* to *Bleak House* you can read and laugh and cry and go happy to bed after forgetting yourself in a jolly book. I have pointed out elsewhere how Charles Lever, after producing a series of books in which the old manner of rollicking through life as if all its follies and failures were splendid jokes, and all its conventional enjoyments and attachments delightful and sincere, suddenly supplied the highly appreciative Dickens (as editor of *All the Year Round*) with a quite new sort of novel, called *A Day's Ride: A Life's Romance*,[14] which affected both Dickens and the public very unpleasantly by the bitter but tonic flavor we now know as Ibsenism; for the hero began as that uproarious old joke, the boaster who, being a coward, is led into all sorts of dangerous situations, like Bob Acres[15] and Mr. Winkle, and then unexpectedly made them laugh very much on the wrong side of their mouths, exactly as if he were a hero by Ibsen, Strindberg, Turgenieff, Tolstoy, Gorki, Tchekov, or Brieux. And here there was no question of the author being taken too gloomily. His readers, full of Charles O'Malley and Mickey Free,[16] were approaching the work with the most unsuspicious confidence in its entire jollity. The shock to the security of their senseless laughter caught them utterly unprepared; and they resented it accordingly.

Now that a reaction against realism has set in, and the old jolly ways are coming into fashion again, it is perhaps not so easy as it once was to conceive the extraordinary fascination of this mirthless comedy, this tragedy that stripped the soul naked instead of bedizening it in heroic trappings. But if you have not experienced this fascination yourself, and cannot conceive it, you may take my word for it that it exists, and operates with such power that it puts Shakespear himself out of countenance. And even for those who are

[14]Lever's *A Day's Ride* was published in *All the Year Round* from 18 August 1860 to 23 March 1861.
[15]A character in Richard Brinsley Sheridan's *The Rivals* (1775).
[16]Characters in Charles Lever's novel *Charles O'Malley, the Irish Dragoon* (1841).

in full reaction against it, it can hardly be possible to go back from the death of Hedwig Ekdal to the death of Little Nell otherwise than as a grown man goes down on all fours and pretends to be a bear for the amusement of his children. Nor need we regret this: there are noble compensations for our increase of wisdom and sorrow. After Hedwig you may not be able to cry over Little Nell, but at least you can read *Little Dorrit* without calling it twaddle, as some of its first critics did. The jests do not become poorer as they mature into earnest. It was not through joyless poverty of soul that Shelley never laughed, but through an enormous apprehension and realization of the gravity of things that seemed mere fun to other men. If there is no Swiveller and no Trabb's boy in *The Pilgrim's Progress,* and if Mr. Badman is drawn as Ibsen would have drawn him and not as Sheridan would have seen him, it does not follow that there is less strength (and joy is a quality of strength) in Bunyan than in Sheridan and Dickens. After all, the salvation of the world depends on the men who will not take evil good-humoredly, and whose laughter destroys the fool instead of encouraging him. "Rightly to be great," said Shakespear when he had come to the end of mere buffoonery, "is greatly to find quarrel in a straw."[17] The English cry of "Amuse us: take things easily: dress up the world prettily for us" seems mere cowardice to the strong souls that dare look facts in the face; and just so far as people cast off levity and idolatry they find themselves able to bear the company of Bunyan and Shelley, of Ibsen and Strindberg and the great Russian realists, and unable to tolerate the sort of laughter that African tribes cannot restrain when a man is flogged or an animal trapped and wounded. They are gaining strength and wisdom: gaining, in short, that sort of life which we call the life everlasting, a sense of which is worth, for pure well-being alone, all the brutish jollities of Tom Cringle and Humphrey Clinker, and even of Falstaff, Pecksniff, and Micawber.

[17]*Hamlet,* IV.iv.53–55.

'GREAT EXPECTATIONS

BY CHARLES DICKENS

WITH A ~~NEW~~ PREFACE BY BERNARD SHAW

~~AND~~ ILLUSTRATIONS BY GORDON ROSS

TITLE PAGE BY JOHN FARLEIGH

We must put all this in a slipform, I think.

This looks as if the man were hiding a hush behind him.

The boy is a David Copperfield boy, not a Gatesmith apprentice

EDINBURGH
PRINTED FOR THE MEMBERS OF THE LIMITED EDITIONS CLUB BY
R. & R. CLARK LIMITED
1937

This page arose out of Shaw's idea that Farleigh should do the title page. He got G.B.S. to abandon the notion

This is the young blacksmith wishing he were not a common boy and fit to marry Estella. Expense had moulded.

Foreword to *Great Expectations*

A revised text published in 1947 by Hamish Hamilton (London) in the Novel Library. Originally published as a preface to an edition issued by the Limited Editions Club (New York) in 1937.

Great Expectations is the last of the three full-length stories written by Dickens in the form of an autobiography. Of the three, *Bleak House,* as the autobiography of Miss Esther Summerson, is naturally the least personal, as Esther is not only a woman but a maddening prig, though we are forced to admit that such paragons exist and are perhaps worthy of the reverent admiration with which Dickens regarded them. Ruling her out, we have *David Copperfield* and *Great Expectations.* David was, for a time at least, Dickens's favourite child, perhaps because he had used him to express the bitterness of that episode in his own experience which had wounded his boyish self-respect most deeply. For Dickens, in spite of his exuberance, was a deeply reserved man: the exuberance was imagination and acting (his imagination was ceaseless, and his outward life a feat of acting from beginning to end); and we shall never know whether in that immensely broadened outlook and knowledge of the world which began with *Hard Times* and *Little Dorrit,* and left all his earlier works behind, he may not have come to see that making his living by sticking labels on blacking bottles and rubbing shoulders with boys who were not gentlemen, was as little shameful as being the genteel apprentice in the office of Mr. Spenlow, or the shorthand writer recording the unending twaddle of the House of Commons and electioneering bunk on the hustings of all the Eatanswills in the country.

That there was a tragic change in his valuations can be shown by contrasting Micawber with William Dorrit, in which light Micawber suddenly becomes a mere marionette pantaloon with a funny bag of tricks which he repeats until we can bear no more of him, and Dorrit a portrait of the deadliest and deepest truth to nature. Now contrast David with Pip; and believe, if you can, that there was no revision of his estimate of the favorite child David as a work of art and even as a vehicle of experience. The adult David fades into what stage managers call a walking gentleman. The reappearance of Mr. Dickens in the character of a blacksmith's boy may be regarded as an apology to Mealy Potatoes [in *David Copperfield*].

Dickens did in fact know that *Great Expectations* was his most compactly perfect book. In all the other books, there are episodes of wild extravagance, extraordinarily funny if they catch you at the right age, but recklessly grotesque as nature studies. Even in *Little Dorrit*, Dickens's masterpiece among many masterpieces, it is impossible to believe that the perfectly authentic Mr. Pancks really stopped the equally authentic Mr. Casby in a crowded street in London and cut his hair; and though Mr. F.'s aunt is a first-rate clinical study of senile deficiency in a shrewd old woman, her collisions with Arthur Clennam are too funny to be taken seriously. We cannot say of Casby, Pancks, and the aunt, as we can say of Sam Weller, that such people never existed; for most of us have met their counterparts in real life; but we can say that Dickens's sense of fun ran away with him over them. If we have absolutely no fun in us we may even state gravely that there has been a lapse from the artistic integrity of the tragic picture of English society which is the subject of the book.

In *Great Expectations* we have Wopsle and Trabb's boy; but they have their part and purpose in the story and do not overstep the immodesty of nature. It is hardly decent to compare Mr. F.'s aunt with Miss Havisham; but as contrasted studies of madwomen they make you shudder at the thought of what Dickens might have made of Miss Havisham if he had seen her as a comic personage. For life is no laughing matter in *Great Expectations*; the book is all-of-one piece and consistently truthful as none of the other books are, not even the compact *Tale of Two Cities*, which is pure sentimental melodrama from beginning to end, and shockingly wanting in any philosophy of history in its view of the French Revolution.

Dickens never regarded himself as a revolutionist, though he certainly was one. His implacable contempt for the House of Commons, founded on his experience as parliamentary reporter, never wavered from the account of the Eatanswill election and of Nicholas Nickleby's interview with Pugstyles to the Veneering election in *Our Mutual Friend*, his last book (*Edwin Drood* is only a gesture by a man three-quarters dead). And this was not mere satire, of which there had been plenty. Dickens was the first writer to perceive and state definitely that the House of Commons, working on the Party system, is an extraordinarily efficient device for dissipating all our reforming energy and ability in Party debate and when anything urgently needs to be done, finding out "how not to do it." It took very little time to get an ineffective Factory Act. It took fifty years to make it effective, though the labour conditions in the factories and mines were horrible. After Dickens's death, it took thirty years to pass an Irish Home Rule Bill, which was promptly repudiated by the military plutocracy, leaving the question to be settled by a competition in slaughter and house burning, just as it would have been between two tribes of savages. Liberty under the British parliamentary system means slavery for nine-tenths of the people, and slave exploitation or parasitic idolatry and snobbery for the rest. Parliament men—one cannot call them statesmen—and even historians, keep declaring that the British parliamentary system is one of the greatest blessings British political genius has given to the world; and the world has taken it at its self-valuation and set up imitations of it all over Europe and America, always with the same result: political students outside Parliament exposing the most frightful social evils and prescribing their remedies, and Parliament ignoring them as long as possible and then engulfing their disciples and changing them from reformers into partisans with time for nothing but keeping their party in power or opposing the Government, rightly or wrongly ("it is the duty of the Opposition to oppose"),[1] as the case might be. In the middle of the nineteenth century Dickens saw this and said it. He had to be ignored, as he would not stand for Parliament and be paralyzed.

Europe has had to learn from hard experience what it would not learn from Dickens. The Fascist and Communist revolutions which swept the great parliamentary sham into the dustbin after it had produced a colossal Anarchist war, made no mention of Dickens; but on the parliamentary point he was as much their prophet as Marx was the economic prophet of the Soviets. Yet a recent reac-

---

[1]Credited to Lord Randolph S. Churchill, 1830, but allegedly quoted by him from an earlier parliamentary speech by the statesman George Tierney (1761–1830), vehement opponent of the prime minister, William Pitt.

tionist against Dickens worship declares that he "never went ahead of his public."[2]

Marx and Dickens were contemporaries living in the same city and pursuing the same profession of literature; yet they seem to us like creatures of a different species living in different worlds. Dickens, if he had ever become conscious of Karl Marx, would have been classed with him as a revolutionist. The difference between a revolutionist and what Marx called a bourgeois is that the bourgeois regards the existing social order as the permanent and natural order of human society, needing reforms now and then and here and there, but essentially good and sane and right and respectable and proper and everlasting. To the revolutionist it is transitory, mistaken, objectionable, and pathological: a social disease to be cured, not to be endured. We have only to compare Thackeray and Trollope with Dickens to perceive this contrast. Thackeray reviled the dominant classes with a savagery which would have been unchivalrous in Dickens: he denied to his governing class characters even the common good qualities and accomplishments of ladies and gentlemen, making them mean, illiterate, dishonest, ignorant, sycophantic to an inhuman degree, whilst Dickens, even when making his aristocrats ridiculous and futile, at least made gentlemen of them. Trollope, who regarded Thackeray as his master and exemplar, had none of his venom, and has left us a far better balanced and more truthful picture of Victorian well-off society, never consciously whitewashing it, though allowing it its full complement of black sheep of both sexes. But Trollope's politics were those of the country house and the hunting field just as were Thackeray's. Accordingly, Thackeray and Trollope were received and approved by fashionable society with complete confidence. Dickens, though able to fascinate all classes, was never so received or approved except by quite goodnatured or stupid ladies and gentlemen who were incapable of criticizing anyone who could make them laugh and cry. He was told that he could not describe a gentleman and that *Little Dorrit* is twaddle. And the reason was that in his books the west-end heaven appears as a fool's paradise that must pass away instead of being an indispensable preparatory

[2]Hugh Kingsmill, *The Sentimental Journey: A Life of Dickens* (1934). See Part II, below, p. 82.

school for the New Jerusalem of Revelation. A leading encyclopedia tells us that Dickens had "no knowledge of country gentlemen." It would have been nearer the mark to say that Dickens knew all that really mattered about Sir Leicester Dedlock and that Trollope knew nothing that really mattered about him. Trollope and Thackeray could see Chesney Wold; but Dickens could see through it. And this was no joke to Dickens. He was deeply concerned about it, and understood how revolutions begin with burning the chateaux.

The difference between Marx and Dickens was that Marx knew that he was a revolutionist whilst Dickens had not the faintest suspicion of that part of his calling. Compare the young Dickens looking for a job in a lawyer's office and teaching himself shorthand to escape from his office stool to the reporters' gallery, with the young Trotsky, the young Lenin, quite deliberately facing disreputable poverty and adopting revolution as their profession with every alternative of bourgeois security and respectability much more fully open to them than to Dickens.

And this brings us to Dickens's position as a member of the educated and cultured classes who had neither education nor culture. This was fortunate for him and for the world in one way, as he escaped the school and university routine which complicates cultural Philistinism with the mentality of a Red Indian brave. Better no schooling at all than the schooling of Rudyard Kipling and Winston Churchill. But there are homes in which a mentally acquisitive boy can make contact with the fine arts. I myself learnt nothing at school, but gained in my home an extensive and highly educational knowledge of music. I had access to illustrated books on painting which sent me to the National Gallery[3]; so that I was able to support myself as a critic of music and painting as Dickens supported himself by shorthand. I devoured books on science and on the religious controversies of the day. It is in this way, and not in our public schools and universities that such culture as there is in England is kept alive.

Now the Dickenses seem to have been complete barbarians. Dickens mentions the delight with which he discovered in an attic a heap of eighteenth-century novels. But Smollett was a grosser barbarian than Dickens himself; and *Don Quixote* and *The Arabian*

[3]This was, of course, the National Gallery of Ireland, in Dublin.

Nights, though they gave the cue to his eager imagination, left him quite in the dark as to the philosophy and art of his day. To him a philosopher, an intellectual, was a figure of fun. Count Smorltork is the creation by a street Arab: Dickens did not even know that the Count's method of studying Chinese metaphysics by studying metaphysics and China and "combining the information" was not only sensible and correct, but the only possible method. To Dickens as to most Victorian Englishmen metaphysics were ridiculous, useless, unpractical, and the mark of a fool. He was musical enough to have a repertory of popular ballads which he sang all over the house to keep his voice in order; and he made Tom Pinch play the organ in church as an amiable accomplishment; but I cannot remember hearing that he ever went to a classical concert, or even knew of the existence of such entertainments. The articles on the National Gallery [London], in *All the Year Round,* though extremely funny in their descriptions of "The Apotheosis" of "William the Silent" (the title alone would make a cat laugh), and on some profane points sensible enough, are those of a complete Philistine. One cannot say that he disliked all painters in the face of his friendship with Maclise and Clarkson Stanfield;[4] but it was not a cultural friendship: Stanfield was a scene painter who appealed to that English love of landscape which is so often confused with a love of art; and Maclise was a pictorial anecdotist who presented scenes from Shakespear's plays exactly as they were presented on the stage. When Dickens introduced in his stories a character whom he intensely disliked he chose an artistic profession for him. Henry Gowan in *Little Dorrit* is a painter. Pecksniff is an architect. Harold Skimpole is a musician. There is real hatred in his treatment of them.

Now far be it from me to imply that they are false to nature. Artists are often detestable human beings; and the famous Anti-Scrape, officially The Society for the Protection of Ancient Buildings, was founded by William Morris and his friends to protect ancient buildings from architects. What is more, the ultra-artistic

[4]Daniel Maclise (1806–70), Irish historical painter, provided the frontispieces and titles for three of Dickens's Christmas Books: *The Chimes* (1844), *The Cricket on the Hearth* (1845), and *The Battle of Life* (1846). Clarkson Stanfield (1793–1867), a marine artist who became scene-painter at Drury Lane, provided some of the drawings for woodcuts in the Christmas Books. *Little Dorrit* was dedicated to him.

sets, the Pre-Raphaelites and the aesthetes grouped round Rossetti and Morris and Ruskin, were all Dickens worshippers who made a sort of cult of Trabb's boy and would have regarded me as a traitor if they had read what I am now writing. They knew better than anyone else that Leigh Hunt deserved all he got as Harold Skimpole, that Gowan's shallow sort of painting was a nuisance, and that architecture was just the right profession for a parasite on Salisbury Cathedral like Pecksniff. But all their Dickensian enthusiasm, and all the truth to life of Dickens's portraiture cannot extenuate the fact that the cultural side of art was as little known to Dickens as it is possible for a thing so public to remain to a man so apprehensive. You may read the stories of Dickens from beginning to end without ever learning that he lived through a period of fierce revivals and revolutionary movements in art, in philosophy, in sociology, in religion: in short, in culture. Dean Inge's remark that "the number of great subjects in which Dickens took no interest whatever is amazing"[5] hits the nail exactly on the head. As to finding such a person as Karl Marx among his characters, one would as soon look for a nautilus in a nursery.

Yet *Little Dorrit* is a more seditious book than *Das Kapital*. All over Europe men and women are in prison for pamphlets and speeches which are to *Little Dorrit* as red pepper to dynamite. Fortunately for social evolution Governments never know where to strike. Barnacle and Stiltstalking were far too conceited to recognize their own portraits. Parliament, wearying its leaders out in a few years in the ceaseless drudgery of finding out how not to do it, and smothering it in talk, could not conceive that its heartbreaking industry could have any relation to the ridiculous fiction of the Coodle-Doodle discussions in Sir Leicester Dedlock's drawing-room. As to the Circumlocution Office, well, perhaps the staffs, owing their posts to patronage and regarding them as sinecures, were a bit too insolent to the public, and would be none the worse for a little chaff from a funny fellow like Dickens; but their inefficiency as a public service was actually a good thing, as it provided a standing object lesson in the superiority of private enterprise. Mr. Sparkler was not offended: he stuck to his job and never read

[5]William Ralph Inge (1860–1954) was Dean of St. Paul's, London, 1911–34. The quotation is unlocated.

anything. *Little Dorrit* and *Das Kapital* were all the same to him: they never entered his world; and to him that world was the whole world.

The mass of Dickens readers, finding all these people too funny to be credible, continued to idolize Coodle and Doodle as great statesmen, and made no distinction between John Stuart Mill at the India Office and Mr. Sparkler. In fact the picture was not only too funny to be credible: it was too truthful to be credible. But the fun was no fun to Dickens: the truth was too bitter. When you laugh at Jack Bunsby, or at The Orfling [Clickett] when the handle of her corkscrew came off and smote her on the chin, you have no doubt that Dickens is laughing with you like a street boy, despite Bunsby's tragic end. But whilst you laugh at Sparkler or young Barnacle, Dickens is in deadly earnest: he means that both of them must go into the dustbin if England is to survive.

And yet Dickens never saw himself as a revolutionist. It never occurred to him to found a Red International, as Marx did, not even to join one out of the dozens of political reform societies that were about him. He was an English gentleman of the professional class, who would not allow his daughter to go on the stage because it was not respectable. He knew so little about revolutionists that when Mazzini called on him and sent in his card,[6] Dickens, much puzzled, concluded that the unknown foreign gentleman wanted money, and very kindly sent him down a sovereign to get rid of him. He discovered for himself all the grievances he exposed, and had no sense of belonging to a movement, nor any desire to combine with others who shared his subversive views. To educate his children religiously and historically he wrote *A Child's History of England* which had not even the excuse of being childish, and a paraphrase of the gospel biography which is only a belittling of it for little children. He had much better have left the history to Little Arthur and Mrs. Markham and Goldsmith,[7] and taken into

[6]Giuseppe Mazzini (1805–72), famed Italian patriot, made England his home and London his base of operations from 1837. He and Dickens later became friends.
[7]"Little Arthur" was the pseudonym of Maria Lady Callcott (1785–1842), author of the eight-volume *Little Arthur's History of England* (1835). "Mrs. Markham" was the pen name of Elizabeth Penrose (1780–1837), author of popular school histories of England and France. Oliver Goldsmith (1728–74) wrote *A History of England* (1771).

account the extraordinary educational value of the Authorized Version as a work of literary art. He probably thought as seldom of himself as a literary artist as of himself as a revolutionist; and he had his share in the revolt against the supernatural pretensions of the Bible which was to end in the vogue of Agnosticism and the pontificate of Darwin. It blinded that generation to the artistic importance of the fact that at a moment when all the literary energy in England was in full eruption, when Shakespear was just dead and Milton just born, a picked body of scholars undertook the task of translating into English what they believed to be the words of God himself. Under the strain of that conviction they surpassed all their normal powers, transfiguring the original texts into literary master-pieces of a splendor that no merely mortal writers can ever again hope to achieve. But the nineteenth century either did not dare think of the Bible in that way, it being fetish, or else it was in such furious reaction against the fetishism that it would not allow the so-called Holy Scriptures even an artistic merit. At all events Dickens thought his Little Nell style better for his children than the English of King James's inspired scribes. He took them (for a time at least) to churches of the Unitarian persuasion, where they could be both sceptical and respectable; but it is hard to say what Dickens believed or did not believe metaphysically or metapolitically, though he left us in no doubt as to his opinion of the Lords, the Commons, and the ante-Crimean Civil Service.

On the positive side he had nothing to say. Marxism and Darwinism came too late for him. He might have been a Comtist—perhaps ought to have been a Comtist, but was not. He was an independent Dickensian, a sort of unphilosophic Radical, with a complete disbelief in government by the people and an equally complete hostility to government in any other interest than theirs. He exposed many abuses and called passionately on the rulers of the people to remedy them; but he never called on the people themselves. He would as soon have thought of calling on them to write their own novels.

Meanwhile he overloaded himself and his unfortunate wife with such a host of children that he was forced to work himself to death prematurely to provide for them and for the well-to-do life he led. The reading public cannot bear to think of its pet authors as struggling with the economic pressures that often conflict so cruelly with the urge of genius. This pressure was harder on Dickens than on many poorer men. He had a solid bourgeois conscience which made it impossible for him to let wife and children starve whilst he followed the path of destiny. Marx let his wife go crazy with prolonged poverty whilst he wrote a book which changed the mind of the world. But then Marx had been comfortably brought up and thoroughly educated in the German manner. Dickens knew far too much of the horrors of impecuniosity to put his wife through what his mother had gone through, or have his children pasting labels on blacking bottles. He had to please his public or lapse into that sort of poverty. Under such circumstances the domestic conscience inevitably pushes the artistic conscience into the second place. We shall never know how much of Dickens's cheery optimism belied his real outlook on life. He went his own way far enough to make it clear that when he was not infectiously laughing he was a melancholy fellow. Arthur Clennam is one of the Dismal Jemmies of literature. For any gaiety of heart we have to turn to the impossible Dick Swiveller, who by the way, was designed as a revoltingly coarse fortune hunter, and still appears in that character in the single scene which precedes his sudden appeal to Dickens's sense of fun, and consequent transformation into a highly entertaining and entirely fantastic clown. This was a genuine conversion and not a concession to public taste; but the case of Walter Gay in *Dombey and Son*, whose high spirits were planned as a prelude to his degeneration and ruin, is a flagrant case of a manufactured happy ending to save a painful one. Martin Chuzzlewit begins as a study in selfishness and ends nowhere. Mr. Boffin, corrupted by riches, gets discharged without a stain on his character by explaining that he was only pretending for benevolent purposes, but leaves us with a feeling that some of his pretences were highly suspicious. Jarndyce, a violently good man, keeps on doing generous things, yet ends by practising a heartlessly cruel and indelicate deception on Esther Summerson for the sake of giving her a pleasant melodramatic surprise. I will not go so far as to say that Dickens's novels are full of melancholy intentions which he dares not carry through to their unhappy conclusions; but he gave us no vitally happy heroes and heroines after Pickwick (begun, like Don Quixote, as a contemptible butt). Their happy endings are manufactured to make the books pleasant. Nobody who has endured the novels of our twentieth-century emancipated women, enormously cleverer and better informed than the novels of Dickens, and ruthlessly calculated to leave their readers hopelessly discouraged and miserable, will feel anything but gratitude to Dickens for his humanity in speeding his parting guests with happy faces by turning from the world of destiny to the world of accidental good luck; but as our minds grow stronger some of his consolations become unnecessary and even irritating. And it happens that it is with just such a consolation that *Great Expectations* ends.

It did not always end so. Dickens wrote two endings, and made a mess of both.[8] In the first ending, which Bulwer Lytton persuaded him to discard, Pip takes little Pip for a walk in Piccadilly and is stopped by Estella, who is passing in her carriage. She is comfortably married to a Shropshire doctor and just says how d'y'do to Pip and kisses the little boy before they both pass on out of one another's lives. This, though it is marred by Pip's pious hope that her husband may have thrashed into her some understanding of how much she has made him suffer, is true to nature. But it is much too matter-of-fact to be the right ending to a tragedy. Piccadilly was impossible in such a context; and the passing carriage was unconsciously borrowed from *A Day's Ride: A Life's Romance*, the novel by Lever which was so unpopular that *Great Expectations* had to be written to replace it in *All The Year Round*.[9] But in Lever's story it is the man who stops the carriage, only to be cut dead by the lady. Dickens must have felt that there was something wrong with this ending; and Bulwer's objection confirmed his doubt. Accordingly, he wrote a new ending, in which he got rid of Piccadilly and substituted a perfectly congruous and beautifully touching scene

[8]Shaw's recollection of having read, early in life, a discarded "unhappy" ending to the novel led to a frantic search and an amusing exchange of correspondence in 1935–37 between publisher, printer, and Shaw's secretary, which is chronicled in a brochure *The Mystery of the Unhappy Ending* issued to its members by the Limited Editions Club in 1937. For a comprehensive publishing history and analysis of the two endings, including Shaw's involvement, see Edgar Rosenberg, "Last Words on *Great Expectations*," *Dickens Studies Annual*, IX (1981).
[9]Shaw was in error. *A Day's Ride* appeared uninterruptedly to its end (see p. 43 above, note 14), running, until its conclusion, concurrently with *Great Expectations*, which commenced serialization on 1 December 1860.

and hour and atmosphere for the meeting. He abolished the Shropshire doctor and left out the little boy. So far the new ending was in every way better than the first one.

Unfortunately, what Bulwer wanted was what is called a happy ending, presenting Pip and Estella as reunited lovers who were going to marry and live happily ever after; and Dickens, though he could not bring himself to be quite so explicit in sentimental falsehood, did, at the end of the very last line, allow himself to say that there was "no shadow of parting" between them. If Pip had said "Since that parting I have been able to think of her without the old unhappiness; but I have never tried to see her again, and I know I never shall" he would have been left with at least the prospect of a bearable life. But the notion that he could ever have been happy with Estella: indeed that anyone could ever have been happy with Estella, is positively unpleasant. I can remember when the Cowden Clarks[10] ventured to hint a doubt whether Benedick and Beatrice had a very delightful union to look forward to; but that did not greatly matter, as Benedick and Beatrice have none of the reality of Pip and Estella. Shakespear could afford to trifle with *Much Ado About Nothing*, which is avowedly a potboiler; but *Great Expectations* is a different matter. Dickens put nearly all his thought into it. It is too serious a book to be a trivially happy one. Its beginning is unhappy; its middle is unhappy; and the conventional happy ending is an outrage on it.

Estella is a curious addition to the gallery of unamiable women painted by Dickens. In my youth it was commonly said that Dickens could not draw women. The people who said this were thinking of Agnes Wickfield and Esther Summerson, of Little Dorrit and Florence Dombey, and thinking of them as ridiculous idealizations of their sex. Gissing put a stop to that by asking whether shrews like Mrs. Raddle, Mrs. MacStinger, Mrs. Gargery, fools like Mrs. Nickleby and Flora Finching, warped spinsters like Rosa Dartle and Miss Wade, were not masterpieces of woman drawing. And they are all unamiable. But for Betsey Trotwood, who is a very lovable fairy godmother and yet a genuine nature study, and an old dear like Mrs. Boffin, one would be tempted to ask whether Dickens had

[10]Charles and Mary Cowden-Clarke were joint authors of *The Shakespeare Key* (1879).

ever in his life met an amiable female. The transformation of Dora into Flora is diabolical, but frightfully true to nature. Of course Dickens with his imagination could invent amiable women by the dozen; but somehow he could not or would not bring them to life as he brought the others. We doubt whether he ever knew a little Dorrit; but Fanny Dorrit is from the life unmistakably. So is Estella. She is a much more elaborate study than Fanny, and, I should guess, a recent one.

Dickens, when he let himself go in *Great Expectations*, was separated from his wife and free to make more intimate acquaintances with women than a domesticated man can. I know nothing of his adventures in this phase of his career, though I daresay a good deal of it will be dug out by the little sect of anti-Dickensites whose fanaticism has been provoked by the Dickens Fellowships. It is not necessary to suggest a love affair; for Dickens could get from a passing glance a hint which he could expand into a full-grown character. The point concerns us here only because it is the point on which the ending of *Great Expectations* turns: namely, that Estella is a born tormentor. She deliberately torments Pip all through for the fun of it; and in the little we hear of her intercourse with others there is no suggestion of a moment of kindness: in fact her tormenting of Pip is almost affectionate in contrast to the cold disdain of her attitude towards the people who were not worth tormenting. It is not surprising that the unfortunate Bentley Drummle, whom she marries in the stupidity of sheer perversity, is obliged to defend himself from her clever malice with his fists: a consolation to us for Pip's broken heart, but not altogether a credible one; for the real Estellas can usually intimidate the real Bentley Drummles. At all events the final sugary suggestion of Estella redeemed by Bentley's thrashings and waste of her money, and living happily with Pip for ever after, provoked even Dickens's eldest son to rebel against it, most justly.

Apart from this the story is the most perfect of Dickens's works. In it he does not muddle himself with the ridiculous plots that appear like vestiges of the stone age in many of his books, from *Oliver Twist* to the end. The story is built round a single and simple catastrophe: the revelation to Pip of the source of his great expectations. There is, it is true, a trace of the old plot superstition in

Estella turning out to be Magwitch's daughter; but it provides a touchingly happy ending for that heroic Warmint. Who could have the heart to grudge it to him?

As our social conscience expands and makes the intense class snobbery of the nineteenth century seem less natural to us, the tragedy of *Great Expectations* will lose some of its appeal. I have already wondered whether Dickens himself ever came to see that his agonizing sensitiveness about the blacking bottles and his resentment of his mother's opposition to his escape from them was not too snobbish to deserve all the sympathy he claimed for it. Compare the case of H. G. Wells, our nearest to a twentieth-century Dickens. Wells hated being a draper's assistant as much as Dickens hated being a warehouse boy; but he was not in the least ashamed of it, and did not blame his mother for regarding it as the summit of her ambition for him. Fate having imposed on that engaging cricketer Mr. Wells's father an incongruous means of livelihood in the shape of a small shop, shopkeeping did not present itself to the young Wells as beneath him, whereas to the genteel Dickens being a warehouse boy was an unbearable comedown. Still, I cannot help speculating on whether if Dickens had not killed himself prematurely to pile up money for that excessive family of his, he might not have reached a stage at which he could have got as much fun out of the blacking bottles as Mr. Wells got out of his abhorred draper's counter.

Dickens never reached that stage; and there is no prevision of it in *Great Expectations*; for in it he never raises the question why Pip should refuse Magwitch's endowment and shrink from him with such inhuman loathing. Magwitch no doubt was a Warmint from the point of view of the genteel Dickens family and even from his own; but Victor Hugo would have made him a magnificent hero, another Valjean. Inspired by an altogether noble fixed idea, he had lifted himself out of his rut of crime and honestly made a fortune for the child who had fed him when he was starving. If Pip had no objection to be a parasite instead of an honest blacksmith, at least he had a better claim to be a parasite on Magwitch's earnings than, as he imagined, on Miss Havisham's property. It is curious that this should not have occurred to Dickens; for nothing could exceed the bitterness of his exposure of the futility of Pip's parasitism. If all that came of sponging on Miss Havisham (as he thought) was the privilege of being one of the Finches of the Grove, he need not have felt his dependence on Magwitch to be incompatible with his entirely baseless self-respect. But Pip—and I am afraid Pip must be to this extent identified with Dickens—could not see Magwitch as an animal of the same species as himself or Miss Havisham. His feeling is true to the nature of snobbery; but his creator says no word in criticism of that ephemeral limitation.

The basic truth of the situation is that Pip, like his creator, has no culture and no religion. Joe Gargery, when Pip tells a monstrous string of lies about Miss Havisham, advises him to say a repentant word about it in his prayers; but Pip never prays; and church means nothing to him but Mr. Wopsle's orotundity. In this he resembles David Copperfield, who has gentility but neither culture nor religion. Pip's world is therefore a very melancholy place, and his conduct, good or bad, always helpless. This is why Dickens worked against so black a background after he was roused from his ignorant middle-class cheery optimism by Carlyle. When he lost his belief in bourgeois society and with it his lightness of heart he had neither an economic Utopia nor a credible religion to hitch on to. His world becomes a world of great expectations cruelly disappointed. The Wells world is a world of greater and greater expectations continually being fulfilled. This is a huge improvement. Dickens never had time to form a philosophy or define a faith; and his later and greater books are saddened by the evil that is done under the sun; but at least he preserved his intellectual innocence sufficiently to escape the dismal pseudo-scientific fatalism that was descending on the world in his latter days, founded on the preposterous error as to causation in which the future is determined by the present, which has been determined by the past. The true causation, of course, is always the incessant irresistible activity of the evolutionary appetite.

PART II

Correspondence

To Kate Perugini

10, Adelphi Terrace W.C.
2 June 1903 [Burgunder Shaw Collection, Cornell University Library]

[Among the letters written to him by Kate Perugini, Shaw placed a holograph note to indicate that he had burned one of them, in December 1897, at Mrs. Perugini's request. "It contained," he wrote, "an account of her mother, shortly before her death, giving her a box of her father's love letters & asking [her daughters] to read them when she was dead & consider whether they could not be published, to shew the world that Dickens once loved her. When Mrs Perugini read them they proved to her exactly the reverse of what Mrs Dickens gathered from them—convinced her that Dickens, even before his marriage, had given up all hope of finding adequate companionship in his wife's limited sensibilities & outlook. Mrs P's conclusion was that she had better burn them. I energetically dissented & advised her to leave them to the British Museum with a memorandum stating how they came into her possession" (British Library). Mrs. Perugini, having acceded to his advice, now solicited his opinion on another matter.]

My dear Mrs Kate

. . . The question whether you ought to write a book about your father is not an easy one. As a rule a daughter's biography is even less trustworthy than a widow's; and that is saying a great deal. But on the other hand the most violently prejudiced books are often the most useful; for though it is true that there are many things which a prejudiced person cannot see and which a surviving relative mustnt say, yet it is equally true that there are things that only strong feeling can discover and only a surviving relative gracefully admit. To a reader who knows how to allow the proper discount for partizanship partizan documents are much more instructive than academic ones. So if you want to say anything about your father, say it. The one thing I implore you not to do is to write a book about him and leave out all the things you want to say. This is the usual course; and it is a most disloyal one. Unless you are prepared to give yourself away; and to give your sisters and cousins and aunts away; and then—which is perhaps the most startling part of the order—to give your father away, you will produce nothing but some chalk and water which nobody but the kitten[1] will mistake for milk. And that is all I have to say on the subject.

I am greatly pleased at having drawn you decisively on the subject of C.D's appetite. My own theory was that the adoration of turkey and plumpudding was purely symbolic; and I am now in a position to allege this on authority.

At the same time I am not disposed to let him off as a mere teller of stories: all his stories, as stories, were failures; and those which are pure stories and nothing else are not good enough for the Strand Magazine. For instance, compare *Pickwick* with the early attempts to diversify *Pickwick* by melodramatic stories. A few centuries hence all the really able critics will agree that these stories are interpolations by an abysmally inferior hand. The truth is, your father, except when his sense of humor was raging, could do nothing unless his interest was aroused by characters and institutions as factors in society. I could overwhelm you with instances of this if I had space and time before lunch; but I havnt. All I can tell you is that your father was neither a storyteller like Scott, nor a tittle-tattler like Thackeray: he was really a perplexed and amused observer like Shakespear; and if he had frankly borrowed his stories as Shakespear did, instead of laboriously inventing them for himself, his books would have been all the better. His limitation was the Shakesperian limitation: the current philosophies and religions of his day (Great Portland St—Good God!) were perfectly useless to him; and he never arrived at a philosophy or religion of his own. But even this had its advantages; for although it prevented him from understanding things that are intelligible enough to a superior person like myself, it also saved him from cooking his books to fit his philosophy, instead of depending on his enormous power of observation. For instance, the description of Chancery which is the backbone of *Bleak House* is quite invaluable as an sociological and historical document; but if he had been a Fabian he would have regarded Chancery as a secondary phenomenon, and believed that the real evil lay in the institution of property from which all

[1]Frederic George Kitton (1856–1903), author and illustrator, was a Dickensian critic and editor to whom Mrs. Perugini referred disparagingly, in letters to Shaw, as "the kitten."

Chancery suits are derived. The effect of that knowledge on him might have been fatal to *Bleak House*, though it certainly would have been very good for *Hard Times*.

If Swinburne had originated the feeling in his article[2] I could forgive him; but he only spoiled it. William Morris was a tremendous Dickensite; and so were all that set into which Swinburne got planted when he was young. Morris had Trabb's boy on the brain. All the firstrate men are Dickensites just as all the secondrate men are Thackerayites; and Swinburne, to do him justice, was on the side of the firstrate men before he died and was buried, bald headed, in that Putney back garden from which his ghost now breathes alliterative platitudes. *Little Dorrit* is the most complete picture of English society in the XIX century in existence. Ever since it was written history has been proving its accuracy. Colonel North, Hooley, and Whittaker Wright[3] have been caricaturing Merdle; the war the other day revealed a whole group of Sparklers; Leicester Square is full of Rigauds; when you know the Dorrits, Meagles, Casby and Pancks you know five sixths of the English middle class; Mrs Clennam goes without saying; and Bar, Bishop, Mrs Merdle, Mrs Gowan and her son, the Barnacles, the Stiltstalkings and Mrs General are so exact that they have never forgiven your father (and never will) for not taking them at their own valuation. Dorrit's death, beginning at Mrs Merdle's dinner table, is one of the finest strokes of tragi-comedy ever made by a great writer. A man who passes this by as a failure and stops to laugh over a few schoolboy jokes does not deserve that Dickens's daughter should be conscious of his existence—if he can be said to exist.[4]

---

[2]Swinburne's article, "Charles Dickens," first appeared in July 1902 in the *Quarterly Review*, London. It was revised for book publication (1913), edited by Theodore Watts-Dunton.

[3]John Thomas North (1841–96), honorary colonel of the Tower Hamlets Volunteer Engineers, was a noted sportsman whose fortune was derived from speculations in Peruvian nitrate mines. Ernest T. Hooley (1859–1947), a promoter of companies, filed for bankruptcy in 1898. Whittaker Wright (1846–1904), another promoter, was charged in 1902 with financial juggling. Found guilty in 1904, he instantly committed suicide.

[4]This letter brought $3,500 in an auction sale at Sotheby Parke Bernet, New York, on 12 April 1978, the highest sum on record for a Shaw letter.

To G. K. Chesterton

10, Adelphi Terrace W.C.
6 September 1906. [Shaw, *Collected Letters 1898–1910* (1972)]

[Chesterton (1874–1936), popular and colorful man of letters, had
just published a study of Dickens.]

As I am a supersaturated Dickensite, I pounced on your book and
read it, as Wegg read Gibbon and other authors, right slap through.

In view of a second edition, let me hastily note for you one or
two matters.

First and chiefly, a fantastic and colossal howler in the best
manner of Mrs Nickleby and Flora Finching.

There is an association in your mind (well founded) between the
quarrel over Dickens's determination to explain his matrimonial
difficulty to the public, and the firm of Bradbury and Evans. There
is also an association (equally well founded) between B and E. and
Punch. They were the publishers of *Punch*. But to gravely tell the
XX century that Dickens wanted to publish his explanation in
Punch is gas and gaiters carried to an incredible pitch of absurdity.
The facts are: B and E were the publishers of *Household Words*.
They objected to Dickens explaining in *H.W*. He insisted. They said
that in that case they must take *H.W*. out of his hands. Dickens, like
a lion threatened with ostracism by a louse in his tail, published his
explanation, which stands to this day, and informed his readers
that they were to ask in future, not for *Household Words*, but for
All The Year Round. *Household Words*, left Dickensless, gasped
for a few weeks and died. *All The Y.R*., in exactly the same format,
flourished and entered largely into the diet of my youth.

Great Expectations was published in *All The Year Round* (I was
Pip to the life when I first read it) with the unhappy ending, which
will, I hope, soon be accepted as the classic one. The alteration was
made later at Lytton's suggestions, and under economic pressure
probably; but the original version actually got into print and on
record as above.

Dickens's moderation in drinking must be interpreted according
to the old standard for mail coach travellers. In the Staplehurst
railway accident, a few years before his death, he congratulated

65

himself on having a bottle and a half of brandy with him; and he killed several of the survivors by administering hatfulls of it as first aid. I invite you to consider the effect on the public mind if, in a railway accident today, Mr Gilbert Chesterton were reported as having been in the train with a bottle and a half of brandy on his person as normal refreshment.

There is a curious contrast between Dickens's sentimental indiscretions concerning his marriage and his sorrows and quarrels, and his impenetrable reserve about himself as displayed in his published correspondence. He writes to his family about waiters, about hotels, about screeching tumblers of hot brandy and water, and about the seasick man in the next berth, but never one really intimate word, never a real confession of his soul. *David Copperfield* is a failure as an autobiography because when he comes to deal with the grown-up David, you find that he has not the slightest intention of telling you the truth—or indeed anything—about himself. Even the child David is more remarkable for the reserves than for the revelations: he falls back on fiction at every turn. Clennam and Pip are the real autobiographies.

I find that Dickens is at his greatest after the social awakening which produced *Hard Times. Little Dorrit* is an enormous work. The change is partly the disillusion produced by the unveiling of capitalist civilization, but partly also Dickens's discovery of the gulf between himself as a man of genius and the public. That he did not realize this early is shewn by the fact that he found out his wife *before he married her* as much too small for the job, and yet plumbed the difference so inadequately that he married her thinking he could go through with it. When the situation became intolerable, he must have faced the fact that there was something more than "incompatibilities" between him and the average man and woman. *Little Dorrit* is written, like all the later books, frankly and somewhat sadly, *de haut en bas.* In them Dickens recognizes that quite everyday men are as grotesque as Bunsby. Sparkler, one of the most extravagant of all his gargoyles, is an untouched photograph almost. Wegg and Riderhood are sinister and terrifying because they are simply real, which Squeers and Sikes are not. And please remark that whilst Squeers and Sikes have their speeches written with anxious verisimilitude (comparatively) Wegg says,

"Man shrouds and grapple, Mr Venus, or she dies" and Riderhood describes Lightwood's sherry (when retracting his confession) as, "I will not say a hocussed wine, but a wine as was far from elthy for the mind." Dickens doesnt care what he makes Wegg or Riderhood or Sparkler or Mr F's aunt say, because he knows them and has got them, and knows what matters and what doesnt. Fledgeby, Lammle, Jerry Cruncher, Trabb's boy, Wopsle, &c &c, are human beings as seen by a master. Swiveller and Mantalini are human beings as seen by Trabb's boy. Sometimes Trabb's boy has the happier touch. When I am told that young John Chivery (whose epitaphs you ignore whilst quoting Mrs Sapsea's) would have gone barefoot through the prison against rules for Little Dorrit had it been paved with red hot ploughshares, I am not so affected by his chivalry as by Swiveller's exclamation when he gets the legacy— "For she [the Marchioness] shall walk in silk attire and siller hae to spare." Edwin Drood is no good, in spite of the stone throwing boy, Bazzard and Honeythunder. Dickens was a dead man before he began it. [Wilkie] Collins corrupted him with plots. And oh! the Philistinism! the utter detachment from the great human heritage of art and philosophy! Why not a sermon on that?

To Clement K. Shorter

10, Adelphi Terrace W.C.

5 May 1911 [Henry W. and Albert A. Berg Collection, New York Public Library]

[The Dickens House Museum]

[The *Strand Magazine* (London) announced in August 1910 that a Charles Dickens Testimonial Stamp, to be printed by Raphael Tuck, Ltd., would be distributed and sold without profit by the proprietors of the magazine. The object of the stamp, it was stated, was to "rais[e] a fund for the benefit of the descendants of Charles Dickens, and, should the proceeds permit, of in other ways commemorating his memory." Three children and seventeen grandchildren of Dickens presently survived him. "Some of these, bearing his name, are, through no fault of their own, in circumstances which must deeply concern, not to say pain, lovers of Dickens." The sale of stamps would allow all to contribute, whether well-to-do or poor, "without any demand of a charitable nature, without soliciting, without receiving any subscriptions, without acknowledging any subscriptions."

The project received Shaw's immediate endorsement. "Dickens," he wrote to the executive committee (as reported in *The Times* on 1 November 1910), "should have a monument in London like Scott's in Edinburgh. He was a very great writer and a very great man. If the committee would ask the public to set a really magnificent memorial, I should be only too glad to have my name honoured by associating it with the project." In May 1911 Shaw was invited by the Testimonial committee to be a signatory to a letter in *The Times* encouraging the public to invest in the stamps, which could be procured from booksellers and newsagents at a penny each.

Clement K. Shorter (1857–1926), a sponsoring member of the committee, who had written to Shaw to encourage him to sign the appeal letter, was founder (1900) and editor of *The Sphere*. No publication of the appeal letter has been noted.]

I have consented to sign *The Times* letter if a certain sentence in it is altered. I cannot knock into the heads of that Committee the precise nature of the situation. The Dickens stamps may produce

68

any sum from £100 to £100,000. It is therefore of the very greatest importance that, whilst we must use the straits of Ethel Dickens and her sisters to move the public hearts and open the public pockets, we must also be particularly careful not to give the Dickens family a legal claim on the entire sum raised. What I want is a pension for the daughters of Charles Dickens Junior, and then, if possible, a monument to Dickens in London on the scale of the Albert Memorial or of the Scott monument in Edinburgh.

By urging this point, I secured the inscription on the margin of the sheets of stamps which will make it impossible for the descendants of Dickens to claim that the money was raised exclusively for their benefit. But the letter ignores this and re-sets the old trap. I have suggested a simple alteration of a few words which removes this danger.

You say that such precautions are not worth taking because the sum raised will not be more than enough for pensions. But you never can tell. It is true that up to the present all the fanatical Dickensites have been such blighted fools that it seems inconceivable that they should achieve any big success; but if some energetic genius arose who could get these stamps really pushed on the public by news agencies and book-stalls everywhere, more money might come in than you expect. In any case, when a precaution only costs a stroke of the pen, it would be folly not to take it.

Most likely the alternative I suggested will be adopted: I presume you did not see it before you wrote your letter.

To Sir William Robertson Nicoll
[10, Adelphi Terrace W.C.]
4 January 1912 [Humanities Research Center, University of Texas at Austin]

[Sir William Nicoll (1851–1923), founder and editor of *The Book-man* (London), informed Shaw on 2 January 1912 that the February issue would be a special Dickens Centenary Number, for which he was asking representative authors to favor the journal with short notes on: (1) personal recollections of Dickens; (2) indebtedness; (3) evaluation of his novels and consideration of the degree of his appeal to present-day readers. Shaw's replies were hastily penned on the reverse of Nicoll's letter.]

1. None.
2. Obviously a great deal. My works are all over Dickens; and nothing but the stupendous illiteracy of modern criticism could have missed this glaring feature of my methods—especially my continual exploitation of Dickens's demonstration that it is possible to combine a mirror like exactness of character drawing with the wildest extravagances of humorous expression and grotesque situation. I have actually transferred characters of Dickens to my plays—Jaggers in *Great Expectations* to *You Never Can Tell*, for example—with complete success. Lomax in *Major Barbara* is technically a piece of pure Dickens. It is not too much to say that Dickens could not only draw a character more accurately than any of the novelists of the XIX century, but could do it without ceasing for a single sentence to be not merely impossible but outrageous in his unrestrained fantasy and fertility of imagination. No combination of phonography and cinematography could reproduce Micawber, Mrs. Sparsit, and Silas Wegg from contemporary reality as vividly as Dickens; yet their monstrous and sidesplitting verbal antics never for a moment come within a mile of any possible human utterance. That is what I call mastery: knowing exactly how to be unerringly true and serious whilst entertaining your reader with every trick, freak, and sally that imagination and humor can conceive at their freeest and wildest.
3. Dickens was one of the greatest writers that ever lived—an astounding man, considering the barbarous ignorance of his period,

Replies to queries by Sir William R. Nicoll, on Dickens's influence on Shaw and on Shaw's opinion of the value of his novels, for Dickens Centenary number of *The Bookman*, 1912.

which left him as ignorant of Art and Philosophy as a cave man. Compared to Goethe, he is almost a savage. Yet he is, by pure force of genius, one of the great writers of the world. His greatest and deepest contemporaries, Carlyle, Ruskin, William Morris and Tolstoy, knew this perfectly well. All his detractors were and are second-raters at heart.

There is no "greatest book" of Dickens: all his books form one great life-work—a Bible, in fact. But of course the tremendous series of exposures of our English civilization which began with *Hard Times* in 1854, and ended with *Our Mutual Friend*, threw his earlier works, entertaining as they are, into the shade. *Little Dorrit* is the work of a prophet—and no minor prophet: it is in some respects the climax of his work. *Great Expectations* is equally wonderful as a study of our individual struggles. But all are magnificent.

To Frank S. Johnson
10, Adelphi Terrace W.C.
12 January 1914 [Henry W. and Albert A. Berg Collection, New York
Public Library]

[Frank S. Johnson (1874–1951) was Honorary Secretary of the
Dickens Fellowship (London Branch), which, on 7 January 1914,
had sponsored a "Trial of John Jasper, Lay Precentor of Cloisterham
Cathedral in the County of Kent, for the Murder of Edwin Drood,
Engineer." The presiding justice was G. K. Chesterton. The foreman
of the "special jury" was Bernard Shaw, who, immediately following
the judge's summing-up, rose and delivered the verdict (published in
a transcript of the trial, London, 1914):

"My Lord,—I am happy to be able to announce to your Lordship that we, following the tradition and practice of British Juries,
have arranged our verdict in the luncheon interval. I should explain,
my Lord, that it undoubtedly presented itself to us as a point of
extraordinary difficulty in this case, that a man should disappear
absolutely and completely, having cut off all communication with his
friends in Cloisterham; but having seen and heard the society and
conversation of Cloisterham here in Court to-day, we no longer feel
the slightest surprise at that. Now, under the influence of that
observation, my Lord, the more extreme characters, if they will
allow me to say so, in this Jury, were at first inclined to find a verdict
of Not Guilty, because there was no evidence of a murder having
been committed; but on the other hand, the calmer and more judi-
cious spirits among us felt that to allow a man who had committed a
cold-blooded murder of which his own nephew was the victim, to
leave the dock absolutely unpunished, was a proceeding which
would probably lead to our all being murdered in our beds. And so
you will be glad to learn that the spirit of compromise and moderation prevailed, and we find the prisoner guilty of Manslaughter.

We recommend him most earnestly to your Lordship's mercy,
whilst at the same time begging your Lordship to remember that the
protection of the lives of the community is in your hands, and
begging you not to allow any sentimental consideration to deter you
from applying the law in its utmost vigour."

Shaw's letter survives in a shorthand draft, transliterated by
Blanche Patch.]

. . . It may interest you to know that the day of the trial I
received from Klaw and Erlanger[1] a cable asking me to prepare a

[1]Mark Klaw (1858–1936) and A. L. Erlanger (1860–1930) were American theater
managers in partnership, rivaled only by the Shuberts.

version of the trial for the stage. This was on the strength of the cabled Press reports, which must have therefore been favourable.

I thought a good deal of the trial was dull, not unavoidably so. A series of trials might be given with success—of Pecksniff for hypocrisy, of Micawber for obtaining loans under false pretenses, of Esther Summerson for being a prig who is not able to know suitable rules: the chief of which should be that witnesses should not be taken through the official document but only cross examined on it; that the audience should be treated as the Jury and given voting papers; and that the Judge should enforce the time limits as if he were a chairman.

To The Editor of the Newsletter of the Sheffield Branch Of the Dickens Fellowship
[*The Dickensian* (London), June 1914]

I am a Dickensian if by a Dickensian you mean a person who read all Dickens eagerly in his nonage. I read a good deal of him in my childhood before I dreamt of asking whom a book was by. I was a good deal influenced by him. However, I must own that I do not find that cultivated young people in search of interesting novels, can stand Dickens nowadays.

The vogue of Little Nell and Paul Dombey persists only among those who are not likely to count for much in the making of the public opinion of the future: and from the technical literary point of view such slop work as *The Old Curiosity Shop* is indefensible. On the other hand, if you put *Little Dorrit* and *Our Mutual Friend* into the hands of an experienced man of the world who is deeply interested in social questions and behind the scenes in politics, he is startled by the penetration and accuracy of the study of English politics and the picture of governing class life which he finds there.

If Dickens's day as a sentimental romancer is over, his day as a prophet and social critic is only dawning. Thackeray's England is gone, Trollope's England is gone; and even Thackeray and Trollope mixed with their truth a considerable alloy of what the governing classes like to imagine they were, and yet never quite succeeded in being. But Dickens's England, the England of Barnacle and Stilt-stalking and Hamlet's Aunt, invaded and overwhelmed by Merdle and Veneering and Fledgeby, with Mr. Gradgrind theorising, and Mr. Bounderby bullying in the provinces, is revealing itself in every day's news, as the real England we live in.

Ibsen has made short work of Esther Summerson; and no crossing-sweeper now-a-days would marry Agnes Wickfield with a million of her dowry; but we realise at last (Gissing was the first to impress it on us) that Strindberg himself has given us nothing more terrible in his picture of what our civilisation has made of women than Dickens's gallery of shrews and fools from Mrs. Raddle to Mrs. Gargery, from Mrs. Nickleby to Mrs. Wilfer. Dickens's pro-digious command of the tricks by which grown-up children—as we all are more or less—can be made to laugh or cry concealed from his own generation the horror of the exposures he effected of our social rottenness.

His contemporaries perhaps understood " Dotheboys Hall" and Chancery as it is presented in *Bleak House*. They certainly did not grasp the horror of having Mr. Veneering in Parliament, or Mr. Sparkler at the Circumlocution Office. They laughed at Veneering and Sparkler, and did not notice that Dickens was laughing only with one side of his mouth, and was grimly prophetic with the other.

Ruskin and William Morris, great Dickensians both, knew bet-ter and the time is coming when the serious Ruskinian and Morri-sian view of Dickens will take the place of the old, silly, laughing and crying view. I regard the books of Dickens's second period, from *Hard Times* to *Our Mutual Friend*, as of much greater impor-tance than those of his first period. They can be read by thoughtful and cultivated adults as serious social history.

The earlier books are, no doubt, still delightful to simple folk, children, and Americans—who are still mostly villagers, even when they live in cities, but are at least literate, unlike our own villagers, who regard reading (perhaps wisely) as an eccentric, an unhealthy habit. The younger Dickens, for all his enormously entertaining character sketches and his incorruptible humanity and contempt for idolatry, is not guiltless of derisive ignorance and the sensationalism of the police intelligence.

The desperate necessity he was under of providing for a large family, and the barbarous lack of artistic culture which was common to him and to his pretentiously educated rivals, made themselves felt until his social conscience deepened into a point at which any sort of shallowness or insincerity became impossible to him.

In my preface to *Hard Times*, written for a recent edition of Dickens's works, I have emphasized the turning point which this story marks in his development from the satirist and reformer into the conscious and resolute prophet, and in the indulgence of his humor which, always riotous and extravagant, became utterly reckless when he realised that humanity is so grotesque that it cannot be caricatured.

To Alfred B. Cruikshank
[Coole Park. Gort. Galway]
4 October 1918
[Archibald Henderson, *Bernard Shaw: Playboy and Prophet* (1932)]

[Alfred B. Cruikshank (1847–1933), a New York attorney, had sent to Shaw a copy of his just-issued monograph *The True Character of Hamlet*.].

. . . Shakespear, like Dickens, like Cervantes, like most geniuses of their type, made the acquaintance of their characters as they went along. Dick Swiveller on his first appearance is a quite loathsome stage villain from whom the heroine is to be rescued at the last moment. Pickwick and Don Quixote begin as mere contemptible butts, to be made ridiculous and discomfited at every turn. Falstaff is a mere supernumerary butt for the prince and for his philosopher friend Poins (who was to have been the Jaques or Hamlet of the play). But these puppets suddenly spring to life after the first two or three pulls of the strings and become leading and very alive and real characters. . . . This does not happen to uninspired writers, who plan everything laboriously beforehand. If it did, they, taking themselves and their art very portentously, would carefully revise their opening scenes to suit the subsequent development. Not so your Shakespear. He leaves the thing as it grew. I do not defend this carelessness . . . I have been guilty of it myself.

To Gerald Gould

10, Adelphi Terrace W.C.2
25 January 1919 [Burgunder Shaw Collection, Cornell University Library]

[Gerald Gould (1885–1936), poet, critic, and literary editor, was a member of the staff of the national Labour newspaper, the *Daily Herald*, founded in 1912 by George Lansbury. He had just assumed the editorship and was in the process of revamping its operation.]

. . . I have the most dismal apprehensions as to the *Herald* . . . .

The only chance of success is for an editor who can write, and is prepared to kill himself with overwork, to get a staff of men who have never before earned a penny by their pens, and simply edit their stuff until they at last learn how to do it themselves. Dickens did this with *Household Words* and *All the Year Round*, eventually succeeding in training a staff of brilliant, original, whimsical, humorous *nonpareils* who, when he died, were forced to unmask themselves as not having among the lot of them the makings of a decent law stationer's scrivener. You will have to manipulate your puppets as Dickens did; and I wish you joy of your job. . . .

To Merle Armitage

4, Whitehall Court S.W.1
31 July 1929 [Henry W. and Albert A. Berg Collection, New York Public Library]

[Merle Armitage (1893–1975) was an American writer, publicist, and opera impresario. Shaw's letter was inscribed on the flyleaf of a copy of *Little Dorrit* (London: Chapman & Hall, n.d.), containing fifty-eight illustrations by J. Mahoney.]

This is not the original edition of *Little Dorrit*. It is part of an edition in monthly parts which I took in when I was a boy late in the eighteensixties. The illustrations by Mahoney were evidently done in wash, and butchered by the engraver, photographic reproduction being then impracticable. The Barnard[1] illustrations in the other books are much better, as he knew how to draw for the wood.

My acquaintance with the story is of earlier date, as we had at home the first complete issue with the original etchings by Phiz. It is in some respects Dickens's greatest book, following the change to complete seriousness which was marked by his *Hard Times*. The Circumlocution Office has been improved out of recognition by it; but I still meet Mr. Sparkler in all directions, and Merdles by the dozen, though they unfortunately don't commit suicide.

My old friend and political colleague Sidney Webb, now Lord Passfield,[2] also had his mind formed in youth by another copy of the Phiz *Little Dorrit* which his parents left lying about.

[1]Frederick Barnard (1846–96), black and white artist, created the illustrations for the Illustrated Household Edition (1871–79) of Dickens's works.
[2]Sidney Webb (1859–1947), 1st Baron Passfield, was Shaw's close associate in the Fabian Society, from 1884.

To The Editor of *Time and Tide*

[" 'This Ever-Diverse Pair' ," *Time and Tide* (London),
27 July 1935]

Sir—My excuse for butting into this controversy is that I happen to be responsible for the preservation of Dickens's letters to his
wife, and their deposition in the British Museum.

Shortly after the death of Mrs. Dickens, her daughter Kate
(Mrs. Perugini) came to me in distress of mind for advice. Her case
was that Mrs. Dickens, about a year before her death, had brought
her a box containing all Dickens's letters to his wife. Her instruc-
tions were that Mrs. Perugini, after her mother's death, was to read
the letters and consider whether they should not be published with
the object of showing "that your father really loved me."

From time to time after this, Mrs. Dickens asked whether the
box was safe in Mrs. Perugini's custody. On being reassured, she
said no more on the subject.

Then Mrs. Dickens died; and Kate opened the box and read the
letters. This she did with the greatest reluctance; for she was a
sensitive soul, and shrank from reading sacredly private letters that
were not meant for her eyes. However, she had to read them; and
the interpretation she placed on them was that her mother was
completely deluded, and that what they really proved was that
Dickens had never loved his wife, and had found out his mistake
even before their marriage. It seemed to her that her duty was to
burn the letters; but before taking this extreme step she wanted to
be fortified by my advice. She had talked about her father to me,
and tried to impress me with the tragic situation of a man of genius
imbedded in a large family of perfectly commonplace persons.

However, I surprised her by telling her that on no account must
she burn the letters. I did not question her report of their contents;
but I pointed out that the sentimental sympathy of the nineteenth
century with the man of genius tied to a commonplace wife had
been rudely upset by a writer named Ibsen, and that posterity might
sympathize much more with the woman who was sacrificed to the
genius's uxoriousness to the appalling extent of having had to bear
eleven children in sixteen years than with a grievance which, after

79

all, amounted only to the fact that she was not a female Charles Dickens. I advised Mrs. Perugini to give the letters to the British Museum, there to abide the judgment of the future.

At first she vehemently objected on the ground that the letters would be exposed in the Museum to the pryings of the Dickens Fellowships and Dickens fans generally, whom she abhorred.[1] I explained that she could put any restrictions she liked on their publicity. I suggested fifty years after her death as a possible date for making the letters public, but urged her strongly to give the Museum Trustees discretionary power in case a heaven born biographer desired access, or on any other serious occasion.

I believe this was the first time her eyes were opened to the fact that there was a case for her mother as well as for her father; and as she had an almost morbid dread of being unjust or ungenerous to anyone, she no longer felt free to burn the letters. At all events she gave them to the Museum with a proviso that they should not be made accessible to everybody until the large family of commonplace persons was extinct. Out of the eleven children only two, herself and Henry Fielding Dickens, delayed this consummation to the scriptural limit. The overcrowded births had mostly shortlived results.

Only the other day I read the letters for the first time, and discovered that it was Mrs. Perugini and not her mother who had been romantically deluded by them. They prove with ridiculous obviousness that Dickens was quite as much in love when he married as nine hundred and ninety-nine out of every thousand British bridegrooms, and that this normal state of things outlasted even the eleven pregnancies.

Exactly what happened then nobody will ever know, except that the initiative in the separation came from the wife, and was long resisted by the husband. She may have been driven crazy by the too rapid exploitation of her fertility; but even if they had had no children, Dickens's continual entertaining of intellectual and artistic people may have been as tiresome to her as life in a sporting

---

[1]Shaw is badly in error here. The letters were deposited in the British Museum in 1899. The Dickens Fellowship was not founded until 1902. Moreover, Kate Perugini could hardly have "abhorred" an organization of which she was a very active President for twenty-five years.

country house would have been to a woman of literary tastes and public interests. Dickens was evidently telling the simple truth when he said that there could not be two people less suited to one another when the babies stopped at last and the pair entered on that phase of life in which incompatibility begins to matter seriously. Dickens's effervescent and histrionic life was not a happy life for his wife. She said so, and asked him to let her go. He resisted until the situation became impossible, mainly, it appears, because separation would shock much the public ideal of his Victorian domesticity.

I once asked the poet, Richard Hengist Horne, who saw something of the Dickens household in the days of the Dramatists' Guild, what he thought of the relations between Charles and his wife. He replied very readily that Charles was very susceptible to anything comic, and that he could not restrain his fits of laughter when Mrs. Dickens's bangles dropped from her fat little arms into the soup with a clink (bangles, or loose Indian bracelets, of which ladies carried as many as they could afford on each arm, were then in fashion). As the Victorians tolerated the sport called making fun of one another to an extent now happily incredible, Horne's reminiscence suggests that Mrs. Dickens may have suffered from a want of respect in her humorous family, especially as the household was run and ruled by her sister Georgina. Dickens noted her cuckoo-like habit of leaving her children to Georgina's care; but one may reasonably ask whether she could be expected to rear them as well as bear them at the rate at which they were produced.

When Mrs. Dickens's relatives began to make mischief about Georgina, and all the Dickenses, big and little, took Georgina's part indignantly, the household blew up; and the too long deferred separation became inevitable. The publication of the letters strips the affair of all mystery. Mrs. Dickens was right: Charles did love her a great deal more ardently than was good for either of them; and so her point is carried and the incident closed. He did not write great literary love letters to her; but what author does play off such professional tricks on his own wife?

If I were a Dickensian ragpicker, I should not bother about anything earlier than the portrait of somebody called Estella in *Great Expectations*. Anyhow, I hope the next editor of his works will restore the original and honest "unhappy ending" of that great work, and discard the scrap of humbug which Bulwer Lytton, in a moment of worldly wisdom, persuaded Dickens to substitute for it.

To Hugh Kingsmill
4, Whitehall Court S.W.1
[Undated: December 1936] [Humanities Research Center, University of Texas at Austin]

[In his preface to *Great Expectations* Shaw was critical of a recent biography, *The Sentimental Journey: A Life of Dickens* (1934), by Hugh Kingsmill (pseudonym of H. K. Lunn, 1889–1949), though he identified it only by cryptic allusion to "a recent reactionist against Dickens worship." In fairness to Kingsmill, Shaw sent him an advance proof of the preface, which resulted in a correspondence between the two writers on the subject of Dickens. Only a fragment of one of Shaw's letters to Kingsmill has come to light, in shorthand draft (transliterated by Barbara Smoker), which frustratingly breaks off in midsentence.]

This is worse than the book. You have allowed your zeal as advocate diabolic to carry you beyond all reason.

What does all the evidence you have hunted out with such admirable diligence come to? Before you produced it we had an entirely goodnatured impression of Dickens's parents. Nobody disliked Mrs Nickleby. Everything was forgiven to Micawber. Miss Beadnell[1] was comfortably immortalized as an entirely kindly and harmless person: nothing worse than a bother. That was the result of Dickens's handling of them. Well, you have revealed and rubbed in the truth about them, which is, that they were utterly impossible as associates for a man of genius, by which I do not mean a person of inexhaustible high spirits and whimsical observation (a Variety

---

[1]Maria Beadnell was a banker's daughter with whom Dickens, at seventeen, fell passionately in love. The relationship continued for four years, petering out in 1833.

Star, in short) but a man with a high sense of values, personal and social.

I took up the cudgels long ago privately for Mrs Dickens as a victim of excessive Victorian childbearing; and I happen to know that she died believing that Dickens had been deeply in love with her when he married her, in which, poor lady, she was quite mistaken. But you and others have shewn that if she had borne only two children instead of ten, she would have been an impossible wife for Dickens. The world did not learn from him that it was his bad luck to have impossible parents, an impossible wife, and—barring Kate and Harry—not very interesting children. It is you who have revealed how much Dickens let the case against him go by default when there was so much to be said for him. Why you have insisted in appearing as a hostile witness instead of a friendly one is for you to explain.

I do not know what you mean by saying that Dickens neglected his children, unless you consider that instead of killing himself as he did by making money to provide for them by frightful overwork he should have spent his time in the nursery with them. Which of them has ever complained of neglect? He actually wrote a very bad History of England for their edification. You have shewn that their mother was too much burdened with their procreation to attend to their education, and that without Georgina Hogarth the household would have been a pretty helpless one; but if Dickens himself had attended to them they would have starved.

What do you think he should have done? What would you have done in his place? You may contend on the strength of his experience that men of genius should not marry, should not have children, should not have parents, either practise birth control or separate their families over several wives like the Latter Day Saints, or half a dozen other interesting proposals. But all you get out of it is the absurd verdict that Dickens was [The draft text ends here.]

To Gladys Storey

[4, Whitehall Court S.W.1]

[Undated: c. 19 July 1939] [Burgunder Shaw Collection, Cornell University Library]

[Gladys Storey (d. 1978), feminist and volunteer worker in both world wars, was encouraged by Kate Perugini to write *Dickens and Daughter* (1939), a book the latter was unable to produce on her own. Shaw, having read the book, wrote at once to Miss Storey to inquire if the account she had given of Mrs. Charles Dickens's death and of the deposit of the letters in the British Museum had originated with the now-deceased Mrs. Perugini. An affirmation of this impelled Shaw to respond with a personal recollection of his long-ago conversations with Mrs. Perugini, which, apart from an inevitable bit of embroidery, was virtually identical with the report in his 1935 letter to *Time and Tide*. The surviving shorthand draft of the letter to Miss Storey, edited here to eliminate the duplicative passages, has been transliterated by Barbara Smoker.]

As Kate decided to tell the story that way, told so it must be in any authorized biography of her, though the untruth-to-nature of Victorian romance is more obvious today than it was in her time.

What actually happened was this . . . . [T]he letters remained sealed in the BM until the death of Henry Dickens, the last and only lucky survivor of Kate's band of brothers and sisters.

They were immediately published[1]; and I read them for the first time. They gave me as great a shock as they had given Kate; for they proved just nothing at all, being the most innocent chops and tomato sauce. Any young man in love might have written them to his fiancée or to his wife. They were like all Dickens's family letters: either chops and tomato sauce or brandy and water: usually both. I was sorry I had not let her burn them. I should certainly have done so if I had read them. . . .

The one thing missing in your book is a photograph of Miss

---

[1]Henry Fielding Dickens, the sixth and last surviving son, died in 1933. The letters were published in 1935 as *Mr. and Mrs. Charles Dickens: His Letters to Her*, edited by Walter Dexter.

Ternan. Is she still alive?[2] I have sometimes wondered where he got Estella from: she must be drawn from the life. Kate was quite wrong about her father knowing nothing about women. . . . [S]he was thinking of Agnes Wickfield and Esther Summerson who were rather irritating idealizations. Estella, who is neither a shrew nor a guy, is ruthlessly true to life.

To The Editor of the *Times Literary Supplement*
["Dickens and Mrs Perugini," *Times Literary Supplement* (London), 29 July 1939]

Sir—Your reviewer of *Dickens and Daughter* bases a strong disapproval of its publication to some extent on a conjecture that Mrs. Perugini's mind, giving way at the end of her long life, upset her judgment as to her mother's wishes.

I had a very serious conversation with Mrs. Perugini on the subject about forty years ago. My last conversation with her took place shortly before her death. Her mind was not in the least enfeebled. It was in the same condition as at the end of last century.

I have no doubt that Miss Storey has carried out the wishes, early and late, of Mrs. Perugini in publishing her book. And I have the best reason for believing that Mrs. Perugini first took up the matter at her mother's request.

The facts of the case may be in bad taste. Facts often are. But either way your reviewer will be glad to have them put right.

[2]The long-suppressed fact that Dickens had indulged for the last dozen years of his life in a liaison with an obscure young actress, Ellen Lawless Ternan, was made public by Thomas Wright in 1934 in a biography of the novelist. As Ellen Ternan was born on 3 March 1839, she would, if still living, have recently passed the century mark. She had, however, died in 1914.

To Anmer Hall

4, Whitehall Court S.W.1

14 November 1940 [Humanities Research Center, University of Texas at Austin]

[Shaw undertook in 1940 to produce, at his own expense, a "keep-sake" for graduates of the Royal Academy of Dramatic Art, for which he provided an unsigned introduction. Proofs were distributed to the members of the Council of Management, eliciting an objection to a reference to Dickens as a heavy drinker by one of the Council-lors, Anmer Hall (theater name of Alderson B. Horne, 1863–1953), actor-manager and owner of the Westminster Theatre.]

I want you to consider the case of Dickens a little before I strike him out at your request. Let me say to begin with that I was brought up on Dickens and have been an ardent Dickensite since I could read.

I do not think the cases of Kean and Robson[1] will bring the danger home as it should be brought home. To our young people they belong to a dead and gone world in which actors were vagabonds who drank like fishes and did not think it mattered. Anyhow the deaths of Kean and Robson at 46 and 43 were nothing like so great a loss as that of Dickens at 58. If Defoe had died at 58 we should never have had *Robinson Crusoe* and the string of famous novels that followed it. He would have been utterly forgotten. If I had died at 58, *Heartbreak House, St Joan* and *Back to Methuselah* would not exist. If Alderson Horne had died at 58, the Westminster Theatre would have been a second rate cinema instead of the home of the best management since Vedrenne-Barker and Shaw at the Court.[2] Think of it.

However, I feel as you do about the passage as it stands. Kean gave way to drink when he discovered on a visit to Jersey that

---

[1]Edmund Kean (1787–1833), unrivaled as a tragedian, was reigning star of the Drury Lane and Covent Garden theaters until his death. Frederick Robson (1821–64), celebrated tragicomic performer, flourished in the 1850's.

[2]John E. Vedrenne (1867–1930) and Harley Granville Barker (1877–1946) were partners in a repertory theater experiment at the Court Theatre, London, 1904–07, underwritten principally by Shaw. A total of 701 performances of eleven of his plays were presented, giving Shaw his first experience of theater popularity.

brandy cost only fourpence a gallon. Robson was an ordinary bar customer. Dickens, not in the least a Bohemian, was landed by his enormous family in expenses which he could meet only by public readings (he was a born actor) in which he had to produce super-human effects in such scenes as the murder of Nancy by Bill Sikes. When he was overworked by this and he found that he had either to stop or live on cocktails, he did not stop. He earned the money; but his next book, *Edwin Drood*, was the work of a dead man. All the old gestures are there; but nobody has ever laughed at Sapsea and Grewgious as they laughed at Pecksniff and Captain Cuttle.

I might substitute Balzac (51) or Oscar Wilde (44); but the effect would not be the same. What I had better do is to enlarge the passage, or append a foot note, so as to distinguish Dickens's case from the others. What do you say to this? . . .

To Anmer Hall
4, Whitehall Court S.W.1
8 January 1941 [Humanities Research Center, University of Texas at Austin]

I have cut Dickens out of the gift book, and substituted a little scientific lecture which is a great improvement; so your remonstrance has been all to the good. . . .

[Dickens] was not a drunkard, though the quantities of brandy and water drunk by the Pickwickians are far beyond anything of the kind now customary. But when his enormous family got him into financial straits, and he found that he could make much more money by his public readings than by his books, he overworked himself desperately, and undertook an American tour when he was exhausted and needed rest very urgently. He could not eat, and he would not stop. He was simply nursed from one reading to the next, and then primed with staggering cocktails (their composition is well known; for he was not in the least ashamed of them) to read the murder of Nancy by Bill Sikes and so forth. He made the money he needed and got through, but only half alive. . . .

To Anmer Hall
4, Whitehall Court S.W.1
22 January 1941 [Humanities Research Center, University of Texas at Austin]

. . . Concerning Dickens, Kenneth[1] told me that you had discovered an American critic who heard Dickens's impersonation of Sam Weller, and discovered that it was neither like Sam nor anyone else on earth. I am not surprised; for Sam Weller never existed nor could exist. He is a delightful fantasy; but on the stage he is impossible: his unreality is exposed at once. Only as a supernatural being, bouncing up through star traps, could he be accepted. The whole book is completely unique and unlike any of its successors.

Dickens does not dramatize well, because his most excruciatingly funny characters do not develop. I have stolen some of them, and I know. The barrister in *You Never Can Tell* is obviously a rechauffée of Jaggers in *Great Expectations*, and he is effective enough; but he has only one entry and one scene. I could not have carried him through a whole play.

---

[1]Sir Kenneth R. Barnes (1878–1957) was principal of the Royal Academy of Dramatic Art from 1909 to 1955.

To St. John Ervine

Ayot Saint Lawrence, Welwyn, Herts.

5 February 1941 [Humanities Research Center]

. . . I drank in Dickens to the dregs in my boyhood. One must agree with Inge that the number of vital public movements that left Dickens untouched is amazing, and that the only thing that interested him in a church was the pew opener. His home life as a child was hopeless. Except for a bundle of old novels, by Smollett and that lot, which he found in a garret, he had no contacts with music or art or philosophy of any kind. His ignorance was stupendous. The only thing he learnt was shorthand to make himself a verbatim reporter; and as a reporter he acquired a contempt for our parliamentary machine which never relaxed from Eatanswill in *Pickwick* to Veneering in *Our Mutual Friend*. Curiously, both [Sidney] Webb and myself were brought up on *Little Dorrit*, a volume of which with the old illustrations happened to be lying about in both our houses; and though the How Not To Do It chapters ought to have warned us not to waste our time in forming a Labor Party in Parliament it was not until we had seen what became of that Party under the leadership of MacDonald[1] and witnessed how it changed him from an ultra-intransigent Socialist into a sold-out bunk merchant that we began to realize how right Dickens was, though unfortunately he could only observe the fact, and could not explain it or give the history of the trick by which Sunderland[2] taught William III how to spiflicate the victorious Parliament.

All the same, Dickens, who was as full of social compunction as his contemporary Karl Marx, became a changed man when Carlyle and Ruskin opened his eyes to the condition of the proletariat, of which he knew nothing but what he had picked up in the streets, in the hotels, and in the kitchen. You have just read *Copperfield*. Well, read its successor *Bleak House*, an Adelphi melodrama complicated

[1]James Ramsay MacDonald (1866–1937), British Labourite, became prime minister briefly in 1924, organizing the first Labour ministry in British history. He served again as prime minister, both in Labour and in Coalition governments, from 1929 to 1935.

[2]Robert Spencer (1640–1702), second earl of Sunderland, was Lord Chamberlain to William III, becoming virtual head of government.

with an attempt to shew that what was wrong with property was the Court of Chancery. Then read *Hard Times*, which is comparatively hard reading, and *Little Dorrit*, a story so great that it is hard to believe that it could have been written by the author of *Copperfield* and *Bleak House*. Compare Micawber with old Dorrit, both modelled on his father. Compare Dora with Flora, who is Dora alive and elderly. Compare the masterly scene where Dorrit, rolling in riches, rises at Mrs Merdle's great dinner party, and makes his old begging speech as father of Marshalsea, with the best page in *Copperfield*; and you will suddenly realize how shallow and immature David's creator was. David writes in the first person, autobiographically. But so is *Great Expectations* [first-person autobiographical]; and again the difference is enormous. Until you have swallowed the later Dickens you do not know of what he was capable.

Pickwick is only the fun of a street Arab. A street Arab of genius, but still a street urchin cocking snooks at the passers-by. There is not a single character in the book, except old Pickwick himself, who even pretends to be real. Sam Weller never for an instant could have existed in this world. Put him on the stage and he is quite impossible. Not even Irving could impose Jingle[3] on an audience as a human being.

Dickens never could repeat *Pickwick* or write anything like it. But the street Arab crops up again for moments to the end of his life. The waiter who ate David's lunch, Mr F's Aunt in *Little Dorrit*, Trabb's boy in *Great Expectations*, are just as outrageously funny as the madman in *Nicholas Nickleby* who said that "All is gas and gaiters," or Sam Weller. Yet Dickens, instead of taking up the small change of realism, discarded it more recklessly. In *Our Mutual Friend*, his last book (*Edwin Drood* is the work of a half-dead man), Silas Wegg says hardly a word that could be uttered by any human being; but he is real right through to the marrow. Bill Sikes in *Oliver Twist* is a stale stage villain. Rogue Riderhood is the very real scoundrel in *Our Mutual Friend*. Yet Bill talks like other people

[3]Henry Irving (1838–1905), who became England's most celebrated actor-manager, first played Jingle in a dramatization, *Pickwick*, at the Lyceum Theatre, London, in 1871. His other stage performances of Dickens included Sparkler, Dombey, Nicholas Nickleby, Bill Sikes, Monks, Leeford, Mantalini, David Copperfield, and Gruff Tackleton.

of his class, whereas Riderhood talks as nobody every talked or ever will talk outside a novel by Dickens. The conversation of Wegg, Riderhood and Mr Venus is the wildest extravaganza; but you know them and believe in them as you cannot believe in the Pickwickians. This, by the way, is thoroughly in the English tradition of Smollett & Co.

Steerforth is nothing. He is all through a boy's worshipped hero and idol; and I think Dickens was quite right to keep him in that cloud-cuckoo-land. The book being written in the first person by the worshipper, this was easy. Steerforth is quite a different job from Miss Mowcher.

Dickens was neither scientific nor godlike with his characters. He hated them and loved them and amused himself with them. The ones he hated he seldom let off without some physical assault or indignity.

The critics used to keep repeating that he could not draw women. Gissing shut them up by asking where they could find a more frightfully lifelike gallery of detestable women, from Mrs Raddle in *Pickwick* to Mrs Gargery and Estella in *Great Expectations*, than Dickens had given them. Esther Summerson and Agnes Wickfield are prigs; but then a prig is only a person who is always more correct and sensible than average human nature can bear. The wise respect prigs. Anyhow, Little Dorrit and Lizzie Hexam are not prigs. . . .

To J. W. T. LEY

Ayot Saint Lawrence, Welwyn, Herts.
20 January 1943 [Present Location Unknown]

[J. W. T. Ley (1879–1943), journalist and editor, was a foremost authority on Dickens and principal spokesman for the Dickens Fellowship in the controversy that had arisen over Dickens's relationship with Ellen Ternan.]

I am in the same position as yourself. Mrs. Perugini discussed her mother's case with me, and was strong on the tragedy of a man of genius with a large family of nonentities; but I never heard of the Ternan lady until Mrs. Perugini was dead, and *Dickens and Daughter* was published. It interested me because the character of Estella in *Great Expectations* suggested that some new woman had come into Dickens's life. She was evidently a portrait. As to Mrs. P. describing him as a wicked man, she may have done so on some particular point in a Pickwickian sense; but she was a thorough Dickensite and not a Kingsmillite, and resented only his preventing her from becoming an actress.

To Leslie C. Staples

Ayot Saint Lawrence, Welwyn, Herts.
5 January 1949 [*The Dickensian* (London), June 1949]

[Leslie C. Staples (1896–1980) was editor of *The Dickensian*.]

David Copperfield, once Dickens's pet book, was wiped out by *Great Expectations*, much as Dora was wiped out by Flora, and Little Em'ly left as dead as a door-nail.

Note that though Dickens always insisted rightly that there are villains in the world (Murdstones and Carkers and Blandoises) there is no villain in *Great Expectations*. The convict is redeemed like Victor Hugo's criminal [Jean Valjean] in *Les Miserables*. And the Agnes Wickfields and Esther Summersons give place to a quite new and unDickensish Estella, not yet identified, whom he must have met after his separation from his wife.

There is a lot more to be said about David; but I have no time to say it.

PART III

Dickensian
Shavings

Romantic Fisticuffs and Poetic Justice

[Extract from the preface to *Cashel Byron's Profession* (1886)]

I need not postpone a comment on the vast propaganda of pugnacity in modern fiction; a propaganda that must be met, not by shocked silence, but by counter-propaganda. And this counter-propaganda must not take the usual form of "painting the horrors." Horror is fascinating: the great criminal is always a popular hero. People are seduced by romance because they are ignorant of reality; and this is as true of the prize ring as of the battlefield. The intelligent prizefighter is not a knight-errant: he is a disillusioned man of business trying to make money at a certain weight and at certain risks, not of bodily injury (for a bruise is soon cured), but of pecuniary loss. When he is a Jew, a negro, a gypsy, or a recruit from that gypsified, nomadic, poaching, tinkering, tramping class which exists in all countries, he differs from the phlegmatic John Bull pugilist (an almost extinct species) exactly as he would differ from him in any other occupation: that is, he is a more imaginative liar, a more obvious poser, a more plausible talker, a vainer actor, a more reckless gambler, and more easily persuaded that he is beaten or even killed when he has only received an unusually hard punch. The unintelligent prizefighter is often the helpless tool of a gang of gamblers, backers, and showmen, who set him on to fight as they might set on a dog. And the spectacle of a poor human animal fighting faithfully for his backers, like a terrier killing rats, or a racehorse doing its best to win a race for its owner, is one which ought to persuade any sensible person of the folly of treating the actual combatants as "the principals" in a prizefight. Cockfighting was not suppressed by imprisoning the cocks; and prizefighting will not be suppressed by imprisoning the pugilists. But, intelligent or unintelligent, first rate like Cashel Byron, second rate like Skene,[1] or third rate like William Paradise[2] in this story, the prizefighter is no more what the spectators imagine him to be than the lady with

[1] Ned Skene, in *Cashel Byron's Profession*, is former champion of England, who runs a boxing academy in Melbourne, Australia.

[2] A prizefighter against whom Shaw's pugilist protagonist, Cashel Byron, wages his last fight.

the wand and star in the pantomine is really a fairy queen. And since *Cashel Byron's Profession*, on its prizefighting side, is an attempt to take the reader behind the scenes without unfairly confusing professional pugilism with the blackguardly environment which is no more essential to it than to professional cricket, and which is now losing its hold on the pugilist through the substitution of gate-money at boxing exhibitions for stakes at prizefights as his means of living, I think I may let it go its way with a reasonable prospect of seeing it do more good than harm.

It may even help in the Herculean task of eliminating romantic fisticuffs from English novels, and so clear them from the reproach of childishness and crudity which they certainly deserve in this respect. Even in the best nineteenth century novels the heroes knock the villains down. Bulwer Lytton's Kenelm Chillingly[3] was a 'scientific' pugilist, though his technique will hardly be recognized by experts. Thackeray, who, when defeated in a parliamentary election, publicly compared himself to Gregson beaten by Gully,[4] loved a fight almost as much as he loved a fool. Even the great Dickens himself never quite got away from this sort of schoolboyishness; for though Joe Gargery knocking down Orlick is much more plausible than Oliver Twist punching the head of Noah Claypole, still the principle is the same: virtue still insists on victory, domination, and triumphant assault and battery. It is true that *Dombey and Son* contains a pious attempt to caricature a prizefighter; but no qualified authority will pretend that Dickens caught The [Game] Chicken's point of view, or did justice to the social accomplishments of the ring. Mr Toots's silly admiration of the poor boxer, and the manner in which the Chicken and other professors of the art of self-defence used to sponge on him, is perfectly true to life; but in the real pugilistic world so profitable a gull would soon have been taken out of the hands of the Chicken and preyed upon by much better company. It is true that if the Chicken had been an unconquerable fighter, he might have maintained a gloomy eminence in spite of his dulness and disagreeable manners; but Dickens gave

[3]Protagonist of a three-volume novel *Kenelm Chillingly: His Adventures and Opinions* (1873) by Edward Bulwer-Lytton.

[4]John Gully (1783–1863), later a member of parliament, defeated Bob Gregson in October 1807 (in a fight that lasted thirty-six rounds) and again in May 1808.

away this one possible excuse by allowing the Larkey Boy to defeat the Chicken with ignominy. That is what is called poetic justice. It is really poetic criminal law; and it is almost as dishonest and vindictive as real criminal law. In plain fact the pugilistic profession is like any other profession: common sense, good manners, and a social turn count for as much in it as they do elsewhere; and as the pugilist makes a good deal of money by teaching gentlemen to box, he has to learn to behave himself, and often succeeds very much better than the average middle-class professional man. Shakespear was much nearer the mark when he made Autolycus better company, and Charles the Wrestler a better-mannered man, than Ajax or Cloten.[5] If Dickens had really known the ring, he would have made the Chicken either a Sayers[6] in professional ability or a Sam Weller in sociability. A successful combination of personal repulsiveness with professional incompetence is as impossible there as at the bar or in the faculty. The episode of the Chicken, then, must be dismissed, in spite of its hero's tempting suggested remedy for Mr Dombey's stiffness, as a futile atonement for the heroic fisticuffs of Oliver Twist and Co.

There is an abominable vein of retaliatory violence all through the literature of the nineteenth century. Whether it is Macaulay describing the flogging of Titus Oates,[7] or Dickens inventing the scene in which old Martin Chuzzlewit bludgeons Pecksniff, the curious childishness of the English character, its naughty relish for primitive brutalities and tolerance of physical indignities, its unreasoning destructiveness when incommoded, crop up in all directions.

---

[5]These are all Shakespearean characters: Autolycus a rogue in *The Winter's Tale*, Charles a wrestler in *As You Like It*, Ajax a Grecian commander in *Troilus and Cressida*, Cloten a son of the queen in *Cymbeline*.

[6]Tom Sayers (1826–65), champion English fighter, was known as "The Napoleon of the Prize Ring."

[7]Oates (1649–1705) fabricated a plot by Roman Catholics to massacre Protestants, burn London, and assassinate the king. He was convicted of perjury and sentenced to be pilloried and flogged.

Fiction and Truth

Extract from a lecture, "Fiction," delivered before the Bedford Debating Society, London, on 28 April 1887. First published in *Bernard Shaw's Nondramatic Literary Criticism*, edited by Stanley Weintraub (1972).

It must not be forgotten that writers of good fiction, like all artists who take their art seriously, never quite escape from their apprenticeship until they die or retire from their profession. Their education only ends with their activity. The progress made by the greatest artists during their careers is always so remarkable that no intelligent critic could mistake their early work for their late, or either for that of their middle period. Beethoven's ninth symphony is out of sight of his first. Raphael's cartoons for the Sistine tapestry seem a whole epoch ahead of his Sposalizio.[1] Shakspere's maddest admirer could never have hoped for *Lear* or the *Winter's Tale* from the author of *Love's Labours Lost* or the *Two Gentlemen of Verona*. The difference between the Dickens who wrote *Pickwick* and the Dickens who wrote *Great Expectations* is analagous to the difference between a funny street boy and Schopenhauer. Let me say in passing that the early work is always considered better than the later by the author's contemporaries. Nowadays, however, no artist need start so far back as Dickens or Shakspere. In Shakspere's case there is for this the obvious reason that we are three centuries ahead of him. Dickens was nearer our own time; but he started as an uneducated man. I do not mean, of course, that he was an illiterate man. He could read and write, and had no doubt been taught a little history and geography, the simpler operations in arithmetic, a book or two of Euclid, some Latin grammar and shorthand. He had done much desultory reading and had been through works by such great writers as Shakspere, Bunyan, Swift, and Goldsmith; but he had not a student's knowledge of them, though he had his own peculiar insight to certain sides of them. This was enough to put him on a level as to acquirements with most of his readers. But he was not educated in the sense in which de

[1] Raffaello Santi (1483–1520) painted his "Spozalisio" ("Betrothal of the Virgin") at Perugia, completing it in 1504.

Quincey and George Eliot were educated. No equally gifted man was ever less of an artist and philosopher than he was in 1835 when, in his 23rd year, he wrote the *Sketches by Boz* in a fashion which Bulwer Lytton or Macaulay would have been ashamed of in their teens. He had a shabby genteel knowledge of society, a Londoner's knowledge of outdoor incident, and a reporter's knowledge of public life, besides his genius, which enabled him to succeed easily in spite of the inadequacy of the rest of the equipment. The inadequacy was there nevertheless; and it was the ground of the academic criticism of Dickens as "no gentleman" which persisted long after his great progress made it ridiculous. But at first he seems to have regarded all social phenomena as fortuitous and unconnected; he had neither knowledge of science nor science of knowledge, no philosophy of history, no system of ethics, no grounding of economics, no suspicion of the theories that were behind the abuses he attacked, much less of the social conditions behind the theories; and the gentlemen who were provided with secondhand academic articles of this description despised him accordingly. Much of the abuse he got from them was richly deserved. If his early narrative style could be decomposed so as to separate the workmanship from the fun, and to shade off the reflected felicity of the dialogue, the result would shock his most devoted admirers. His female characters were either purely ridiculous, like Mrs. Nickleby; or awkwardly botched, like Rose Maylie, Madeline Bray, Emma Haredale and the rest; or else, like Mrs. Lupin and Dolly Varden, served up to the reader like the gross feasts of turkey and sausage, pudding, and brandy-and-water which goaded M. Taine[2] to describe him as imbued with the spirit of the English Christmas. Little Nell is of course nothing but a sort of literary onion, to make you cry. The Pecksniff girls shew traces of growing knowledge of female character; but the poor little fool Dora, in *David Copperfield*, was his first distinct success in that department. That was in 1850, in his 8th book, and in his 38th year. Up to that date, and indeed for a few years later, no critic of wide and deep culture could have read Dickens without occasionally being offended and annoyed by his shortcomings. I by no means pretend that all the critics who con-

[2]Hippolyte Taine (1828–93), French philosopher and critic, was the author of the *Histoire de la littérature Anglaise* (1865).

demned Dickens are to be defended on this ground; for the more he improved the less many of them liked him; but I do affirm that his most popular books justified many of the complaints they were met with. His last four completed novels form the only part of his work which placed him above all his contemporaries as a master of fiction. Whether he would have matured sooner had he graduated in the university instead of in the streets may be doubted. Thackeray was a university man; but, as he did not work there, he was fully as ignorant as Dickens when he left it; and he took away into the bargain a class feeling which Dickens escaped. In the slang of our day it might be said that one of these eminent novelists started as a cad; the other as a snob; and that the cad proved the better equipped of the two. In their lack of education proper they were on equal terms. I think they were both the worse for it; and that they blundered and failed in many points to the end of their careers for want of the mental training which de Quincey and George Eliot enjoyed. It will hardly be asserted that George Eliot, as a fictionist, was as gifted as either Dickens or Thackeray. But it will also hardly be denied that parts of her works put parts of theirs to shame in point of intelligence, wise tolerance, and quality of workmanship. She often shewed herself a scientific thinker and a trained sympathiser, where they were only shrewd guessers and vehement partisans.

Dickens's "Third Manner"

Extract from a review of *Jane Annie*, a comic opera by J. M. Barrie and Arthur Conan Doyle, with music by Ernest Ford. *The World* (London), 24 May 1893.

Well, who is the great fountainhead of the modern humorous school, from Artemus Ward[1] down to Messrs. Barrie and Doyle themselves? Clearly Dickens, who has saturated the whole English-speaking world with his humour. We have whole squadrons of humorous writers who, if they had never read him, would have produced nothing but sectarian tracts, or, worse still, magazine articles. His ascendancy is greater now than ever, because, like Beethoven, he had "a third manner," in which he produced works which influenced his contemporaries as little as the Ninth Symphony influenced Spohr or Weber,[2] but which are influencing the present generation of writers as much as the Ninth Symphony influenced Schumann and Wagner. When I first read *Great Expectations* I was not much older than Pip was when the convict turned him upside down in the churchyard: in fact, I was so young that I was astonished beyond measure when it came out that the convict was the author of Pip's mysterious fortune, although Dickens took care to make that fact obvious all along to every reader of adult capacity. My first aquaintance with the French Revolution was acquired at the same age, from *A Tale of Two Cities*; and I also struggled with *Little Dorrit* at this time. I say struggled; for the books oppressed my imagination most fearfully, so real were they to me. It was not until I became a cynical *blasé* person of twelve or thirteen that I read *Pickwick*, *Bleak House*, and the intervening works. Now it is pretty clear that Dickens, having caught me young when he was working with his deepest intensity of conviction, must have left his mark on me far more deeply than on his own contemporaries, who read *Pickwick* when they were twenty, and *Our Mutual Friend* when they were fifty, if indeed they kept up with him

[1]Pseudonym of the American humorist Charles Farrar Browne (1834–67).

[2]Louis Spohr (1784–1859) was a German violinist, composer, and Kapellmeister whose dislike for the late works of Beethoven was well known. Carl Maria von Weber (1786–1826), German composer of the early Romantic period, is best remembered for the opera *Der Freischütz*.

at all. Every successive generation of his readers had a greater advantage. The generation twenty years younger than his was the first that knew his value; and it is probable that the generation which will be born as the copyrights of his latest works expire, and leave the market open to sixpenny editions of them, will be the most extensively Dickensised of any.

Now I do not see why the disciples should not be expected to keep up to the master's standard of hard work, as far as that can be done by elbow grease, which is a more imporant factor in good art work than lazy artists like to admit. The fun of Dickens without his knowledge and capacity for taking pains can only end in what I have called *Jane Annie*—mere tomfoolery. The pains without the humour, or, indeed, any other artistic quality, as we get it occasionally from an industrious "naturalist" when he is not also an artist, is far more respectable. There are a fair number of humorists who can throw off conceits as laughable as Mr Silas Wegg's comments on the decline and fall of the Roman Empire, or his version of "Oh, weep for the hour"! But Wegg himself is not to be had so cheaply: all the "photographic realism" in the world is distanced by the power and labour which gave us this study of a rascal, so complete inside and out, body and soul, that the most fantastic playing with it cannot destroy the illusion it creates.

You have only to compare Dickens's pictures of people as they really are with the best contemporary pictures of people as they imagine each other to be (Trollope's, for instance) to understand how Dickens, taking life with intense interest, and observing, analysing, remembering with amazing scientific power, got more hard work crammed into a thumbnail sketch than ordinary men do into colossal statues. The high privilege of joking in public should never be granted except to people who know thoroughly what they are joking about—that is, to exceptionally serious and laborious people.

Resurrection Pie

Extract from a review of *Jo*, a drama adapted by J. P. Burnett from *Bleak House*. *Saturday Review* (London) 23 May 1896.

At some remote date which I have not precisely ascertained—somewhere between the drying of the Flood and the advent of Ibsen—*Bleak House* shared the fate of most of Dickens's novels in being "adapted to the stage." The absurdity of the process is hardly to be described, so atrociously had these masterpieces to be degraded to bring them within the competence of the theatre; but the thing was done somehow; and the Artful Dodger, Smike, Micawber, Peggotty, and Jo were born again as "famous impersonations." I am less versed in these matters than some of our older critics; but it has been my fate at one time or another to witness performances founded on *Pickwick*, *Oliver Twist*, *Dombey and Son*, and *David Copperfield*. The fame of other adaptations of Dickens reached me, notably that of *Bleak House*, with Miss Jennie Lee as the crossing-sweeper; but I never saw *Jo* until the other night, when Sir Augustus [Harris] revived it at Drury Lane, just as he might have revived [Rossini's] *Semiramide* at Covent Garden. The revival is under the direction of the author of the adaptation, Mr. J. P. Burnett, who has evidently conducted it with the strictest fidelity to its traditions; so that we can now see for a few nights what stage work was like in the days when Dickens, the greatest English master of pathetic and humorous character presentation our century has produced, did *not* write for the theatre. And truly the spectacle is an astonishing one, though I well remember when its most grotesque features were in the height of the melodramatic fashion. What will the stage sentimentalities on which I drop the tear of sensibility today seem like a quarter of a century hence, I wonder!

One facility offered to the stage by Dickens is a description of the persons of the drama so vivid and precise that no actor with the faintest sense of character could mistake the sort of figure he has to present, even without the drawings of Browne[1] and Barnard to help

[1]Hablôt Knight Browne provided 724 illustrations for Dickens's works, from *Pickwick Papers* through *A Tale of Two Cities*.

him out. Yet each attempt only proves that most of our actors either have no character sense or else have never read Dickens. The Drury Lane revival has plenty of examples of this. One would suppose that Mr. Snagsby, with his nervous cough, his diffidence, his timid delicacy, and his minimizing formula of "not to put too fine a point on it," could hardly be confused with a broadly comic cheesemonger out of a harlequinade, nor the oily Chadband in any extremity of misunderstanding be presented as a loose-limbed acrobat of the Vokes-Girard[2] type. Imagine the poor pathetically ridiculous Guster not only condemned to mere knockabout buffoonery, but actually made to fall down in a *comic* epileptic fit on the stage! Bucket has his psychology considerably complicated by the fact that the author has rolled him up with Mr Jarndyce and the Cook's Court policeman; so that there are three characters in one person, a trinitarian expedient which presents an absolutely insoluble problem to the actor. As to Mr. Guppy, he is not within a thousand miles of being himself. What Jobling-Weevle, and Smallweed, and Miss Flite, and George and the rest would have been like if they had been included in the adaptation can only be guessed with a qualm. Literary criticism was more apt to remonstrate with Dickens for caricature than to mistrust his touch as too subtle, and his outlines as too elusive, for the man in the street to appreciate. On the stage, one perceives, Dickens was impossible because he was infinitely too poetic, too profound, too serious, too natural in his presentment of things—in a word, too dramatic for the theatre of his day. Not that I shall allow anyone to persuade me that *Jo* was ever anything more than third-rate work at any period of our stage history; but it must have been much more highly esteemed when it was first perpetrated than it is now, even by an audience invited at "cheap summer prices," and so carelessly catered for, that in the scene in which Guppy explains to Esther Summerson that what she takes for smoke is a London fog, we are treated to the most brilliantly sunshiny front cloth the scene-dock of Drury Lane affords.

All that can be said for Miss Jennie Lee's Jo nowadays is that if the part had been left between herself and Dickens, something

[2]The Vokes family were pantomime artists headed by the dancer Frederick M. Vokes (1846–88). Shaw had first seen The Celebrated Girards at the Alhambra, London, in May 1876, in *Le Voyage dans la Lune*.

credible and genuinely moving might have come of it. But Mr Burnett has carefully laid out his lines and stage business for the crudest and falsest stage pathos and stage facetiousness. Jo is one moment a cheeky street arab, and, the next, is directly expressing, to slow music, not the darkened ideas of Jo, but Mr Burnett's version of the compassionate horror roused in the social and political consciousness of Dickens by the case of Jo and his fellow-outcasts. Dickens himself is not wholly guiltless of this: in the novel one or two of Jo's speeches are at bottom conscious social criticisms; but it is not the business of the dramatist to develop a couple of undramatic slips in a novel into a main feature of the leading part in a play. Lady Dedlock, no longer bored, but fearfully and tragically serious in her crinoline and flounces (wild anachronisms, surely, if the play is to be dated by the costumes of Tulkinghorn, Bucket, and Snagsby), is quite worth seeing, especially on her visit to the graveyard, where she combines a now ludicrously old-fashioned sort of distressed heroine business with a good deal of the Ghost in *Hamlet*, old style. How Miss Alma Stanley has contrived to recover the trick of a vanished stage mode so cleverly, and to keep her countenance meanwhile, I know not. But she does it with wonderful success; and I hope she will never do it again. Mrs. Rouncewell, excellently played by Miss Fanny Robertson, is called Mrs. Rouncell in the playbill; and the number of newspaper notices in which this blunder is reproduced may be taken as the number of critics who have never read *Bleak House*.

Mrs. Raddle's Ibsen: Chuffy and Foldal

Extracts from a review of Ibsen's *John Gabriel Borkman*, translated by William Archer. *The Academy* (London), 16 January 1897.

Our inveterate habit of criticising fiction on the lines of Mrs. Raddle will always get us into difficulties with Ibsen. Mrs. Raddle, it will be remembered, had a fixed conception of manliness which included an instant readiness on the part of every true husband to fight cabmen underpaid by his wife. "Raddle aint like a man," she said, when Mr. Raddle disappointed her in this particular. That is just how we treat Ibsen. We tell each other with great freedom that there is nobody in the world who cannot be done without, and that there are as good fish in the sea as ever came out of it. We even go so far as to say—in French—that in the dark all cats are grey. But we hold that a man should never admit that the world contains more than one possible woman for him: surely a most dismally idiotic doctrine. . . . That is the root objection to Ibsen's people: they will not keep up appearances. They come out with our guiltiest secrets so coolly that we feel that if there were such a thing as a hospital for ailing doctors, and a layman were put into a bed there by mistake, the illusionless conversation in the wards might make him feel as we feel when the old people in Ibsen, long finished with chivalry and sentiment, tell each other the frozen truth about their symptoms.

The fact is, enjoyment of Ibsen is a question of strength of mind. The quantity of truth the average man can bear is still very small; and every increase of the dose is met by piteous protests and cries of "Pessimist," "Cynic," "Morbid," and the like.

The idealists will, of course, take all this iconoclasm as mere satire: Thersites[1] up to date. It is not so: it is sympathy and honesty. The proof is in the result. Compare poor Foldal[2] with any attempt in fiction to get sympathy for an old clerk by the ordinary idealist method of painting out all the selfish spots in him: Chuffy in *Martin Chuzzlewit*, for example. You may wince at every step in Ibsen's process, and snivel with tearful satisfaction at every step in Dickens's; but the upshot is that you are left with a serious belief in and regard for Foldal, whereas Chuffy is nothing but a silly and rather tiresome toy. When Dickens himself, later on, became a serious master of his art, his progress was on the road that leads away from Chuffy and towards Foldal: that is, from sentimental, cowardly, sweet-toothed lying to sympathetic, courageous, nutritious truth.

[1]A "deformed and scurrilous" Grecian in Shakespeare's *Troilus and Cressida*.
[2]William Foldal is an aged clerk in *John Gabriel Borkman*.

Dickens and Shakespear: The Unphilosophic Artists

Extract from the Epistle Dedicatory to *Man and Superman* (1903).

That the author of Everyman was no mere artist, but an artist-philosopher, and that the artist-philosophers are the only sort of artists I take quite seriously, will be no news to you. Even Plato and Boswell, as the dramatists who invented Socrates and Dr Johnson, impress me more deeply than the romantic playwrights. Ever since, as a boy, I first breathed the air of the transcendental regions at a performance of Mozart's *Zauberflöte*, I have been proof against the garish splendors and alcoholic excitements of the ordinary stage combinations of Tappertitian romance with the police intelligence. Bunyan, Blake, Hogarth, and Turner (these four apart and above all the English classics), Goethe, Shelley, Schopenhauer, Wagner, Ibsen, Morris, Tolstoy, and Nietzsche are among the writers whose peculiar sense of the world I recognize as more or less akin to my own. Mark the word peculiar. I read Dickens and Shakespear without shame or stint; but their pregnant observations and demonstrations of life are not co-ordinated into any philosophy or religion: on the contrary, Dickens's sentimental assumptions are violently contradicted by his observations; and Shakespear's pessimism is only his wounded humanity. Both have the specific genius of the fictionist and the common sympathies of human feeling and thought in pre-eminent degree. They are oftener saner and shrewder than the philosophers just as Sancho-Panza was often saner and shrewder than Don Quixote. They clear away vast masses of oppressive gravity by their sense of the ridiculous, which is at bottom a combination of sound moral judgment with lighthearted good humor. But they are concerned with the diversities of the world instead of with its unities: they are so irreligious that they exploit popular religion for professional purposes without delicacy or scruple (for example, Sydney Carton and the ghost in Hamlet!): they are anarchical, and cannot balance their exposures of Angelo and Dogberry,[1] Sir Leicester Dedlock and Mr Tite Barnacle, with

---

[1]Shakespearean characters: the first is the Duke's deputy in *Measure for Measure*, the second a constable in *Much Ado about Nothing*.

any portrait of a prophet or a worthy leader: they have no construc-
tive ideas: they regard those who have them as dangerous fanatics:
in all their fictions there is no leading thought or inspiration for
which any man could conceivably risk the spoiling of his hat in a
shower, much less in life. Both are alike forced to borrow motives
for the more strenuous actions of their personages from the common stockpot of melodramatic plots; so that Hamlet has to be
stimulated by the prejudices of a policeman and Macbeth by the
cupidities of a bushranger. Dickens, without the excuse of having to
manufacture motives for Hamlets and Macbeths, superfluously
punts his crew down the stream of his monthly parts by mechanical
devices which I leave you to describe, my own memory being quite
baffled by the simplest question as to Monks in *Oliver Twist*, or the
long lost parentage of Smike, or the relations between the Dorrit
and Clennam families so inopportunely discovered by Monsieur
Rigaud Blandois. The truth is, the world was to Shakespear a great
"stage of fools" on which he was utterly bewildered. He could see
no sort of sense in living at all; and Dickens saved himself from the
despair of the dream in *The Chimes* by taking the world for granted
and busying himself with its details. Neither of them could do
anything with a serious positive character: they could place a
human figure before you with perfect verisimilitude; but when the
moment came for making it live and move, they found, unless it
made them laugh, that they had a puppet on their hands, and had to
invent some artificial external stimulus to make it work. This is
what is the matter with Hamlet all through: he has no will except in
his bursts of temper. Foolish Bardolaters make a virtue of this after
their fashion: they declare that the play is the tragedy of irresolu-
tion; but all Shakespear's projections of the deepest humanity he
knew have the same defect: their characters and manners are
lifelike; but their actions are forced on them from without, and the
external force is grotesquely inappropriate except when it is quite
conventional, as in the case of Henry V. Falstaff is more vivid than
any of these serious reflective characters, because he is self-acting:
his motives are his own appetites and instincts and humors.
Richard III, too, is delightful as the whimsical comedian who stops
a funeral to make love to the corpse's son's widow; but when, in the
next act, he is replaced by a stage villain who smothers babies and

offs with people's heads, we are revolted at the imposture and repudiate the changeling. Faulconbridge, Coriolanus, Leontes[2] are admirable descriptions of instinctive temperaments: indeed the play of Coriolanus is the greatest of Shakespear's comedies; but description is not philosophy; and comedy neither compromises the author nor reveals him. He must be judged by those characters into which he puts what he knows of himself, his Hamlets and Macbeths and Lears and Prosperos. If these characters are agonizing in a void about factitious melodramatic murders and revenges and the like, whilst the comic characters walk with their feet on solid ground, vivid and amusing, you know that the author has much to shew and nothing to teach. The comparison between Falstaff and Prospero is like the comparison between Micawber and David Copperfield. At the end of the book you know Micawber, whereas you only know what has happened to David, and are not interested enough in him to wonder what his politics or religion might be if anything so stupendous as a religious or political idea, or a general idea of any sort, were to occur to him. He is tolerable as a child; but he never becomes a man, and might be left out of his own biography altogether but for his usefulness as a stage confidant, a Horatio or "Charles his friend": what they call on the stage a feeder.

---

[2]Shakespearean characters: Philip Faulconbridge is a scheming bastard son in *King John*, Coriolanus the patrician Consul in *The Tragedy of Coriolanus*, Leontes the king of Sicilia in *The Winter's Tale*.

Ruskin and Dickens

Extract from a speech delivered at a book exhibition in the Old Bluecoat School, Liverpool, 14 November 1908. *Liverpool Courier*, 16 November 1908.

It is very important to my mind that authors should be original. I do not mean that authors should always say something that has never been said before. One never understands a thing that has not been said before. If a man were to make entirely new observations they would sound so much gibberish, and would mean nothing. It is, of course, inevitable that men with a literary bent should read a great deal, and should form their styles from the reading of the great stylists of the past. But for the matter that they give out, it is of the very deepest importance that they should take that from life, and that they should be sure they are actually dealing with facts and not with romance—and that there should be no foregone conclusion in any department as to morality, religion, or anything else. I will contrast a couple of writers to show the importance of an author's being not only the heir to all the authors who went before him, but also the heir to all the artists who went before him, because we are very largely at the present time under the influence of the authors of the 19th century, and in England unfortunately these authors were the most appalling Philistines—even the greatest of them. I use the word Philistine in the popular sense of a man who knows nothing about art.

Charles Dickens was one of the greatest writers of the 19th century, and one of the greatest writers that England has ever produced. One of the greatest books in the English language is *Little Dorrit*, and when the English nation realises it is a great book and a true book there will be a revolution in this country. One of the reasons I am a revolutionist is that I read *Little Dorrit* when I was a very small boy.

Yet a comparison between Charles Dickens and John Ruskin, another great writer, brings home how astonishingly Philistine Dickens was. He really knew nothing about anything except literature, and that was a very serious handicap to him. One gets a far broader wisdom very often from Ruskin than from Dickens, because Ruskin had been taken all round the world as a child. I have no doubt that Dickens was naturally susceptible to the influence of the other arts, and yet they never reached him because he lived in this Philistine country. Ruskin got his chance, because his father was a rich man—being a wine merchant he naturally would be a rich man.

Ruskin got culture, and Dickens got none, because his father was a poor man, and therefore Dickens was not as a child put into a carriage and driven all through Europe, and shown the most wonderful pictures ever painted. I wonder how many of the young men getting their minds formed in Liverpool—how many of them are getting trained in the way Ruskin was trained instead of the way that Dickens was trained. . . . It is only by having plenty of good bookshops, and first-rate picture galleries, not set aside as a sort of thing for holidays, but as a part of the education of every Liverpool child, with a public orchestra as well to give them constant opportunities of hearing the works of great masters—it is only in that way they will find their future Dickenses growing up with the culture of Ruskin in addition to their own genius.

Poe, Dickens, and the Philistines

Extract from an essay "Edgar Allan Poe." *The Nation* (London), 16 January 1909.

There was a time when America, the Land of the Free, and the birthplace of Washington, seemed a natural fatherland for Edgar Allan Poe. Nowadays the thing has become inconceivable: no young man can read Poe's works without asking incredulously what the devil he is doing in *that* galley. America has been found out; and Poe has not; that is the situation. How did he live there, this finest of fine artists, this born aristocrat of letters? Alas! he did not live there: he died there, and was duly explained away as a drunkard and a failure, though it remains an open question whether he really drank as much in his whole lifetime as a modern successful American drinks, without comment, in six months.

Howbeit, Poe remains homeless. There is nothing at all like him in America: nothing, at all events, visible across the Atlantic. At that distance we can see Whistler plainly enough, and Mark Twain. But Whistler was very American in some ways: so American that nobody but another American could possibly have written his adventures and gloried in them without reserve. Mark Twain, resembling Dickens in his combination of public spirit and irresistible literary power with a congenital incapacity for lying and bragging, and a congenital hatred for waste and cruelty, remains American by the local color of his stories. There is a further difference. Both Mark Twain and Whistler are as Philistine as Dickens and Thackeray. The appalling thing about Dickens, the greatest of the Victorians, is that in his novels there is nothing personal to live for except eating, drinking, and pretending to be happily married. For him the great synthetic ideals do not exist, any more than the great preludes and toccatas of Bach, the symphonies of Beethoven, the paintings of Giotto and Mantegna, Velasquez and Rembrandt. Instead of being heir to all the ages, he came into a comparatively small and smutty literary property bequeathed by Smollett and Fielding. His criticism of Fechter's Hamlet,[1] and his use of a speech of Macbeth's to illustrate the character of Mrs. MacStinger, shew how little Shakespeare meant to him. Thackeray is even worse: the notions of painting he picked up at Heatherley's school[2] were further from the mark than Dickens's ignorance; he is equally in the dark as to music; and though he did not, when he wished to be enormously pleasant and jolly, begin, like Dickens, to describe the gorgings and guzzlings which make Christmas our annual national disgrace, that is rather because he never does want to be enormously pleasant and jolly than because he has any higher notions of personal enjoyment. The truth is that neither Dickens nor Thack-

[1] Charles Albert Fechter (1824–79) was an English actor whose performance of Hamlet, interpreted as a man of action, instigated a great critical controversy.
[2] Thomas Heatherley (d. 1914) conducted a school of art at 79 Newman Street, which Thackeray allegedly used as a model for Gandish's drawing academy in his novel *The Newcomes* (1855).

eray would be tolerable were it not that life is an end in itself and a means to nothing but its own perfection; consequently any man who describes life vividly will entertain us, however uncultivated the life he describes may be. Mark Twain has lived long enough to become a much better philosopher than either Dickens or Thackeray: for instance, when he immortalised General Funston[3] by scalping him, he did it scientifically, knowing exactly what he meant right down to the foundation in the natural history of human character. Also, he got from the Mississippi something that Dickens could not get from Chatham and Pentonville. But he wrote *A Yankee at the Court of King Arthur*[4] just as Dickens wrote *A Child's History of England*. For the ideal of Catholic chivalry he had nothing but derision; and he exhibited it, not in conflict with reality, as Cervantes did, but in conflict with the prejudices of a Philistine compared to whom Sancho Panza is an Admirable Crichton,[5] an Abelard, even a Plato. Also, he described Lohengrin as "a shivaree," though he liked the wedding chorus; and this shows that Mark, like Dickens, was not properly educated; for Wagner would have been just the man for him if he had been trained to understand and use music as Mr. Rockefeller[6] was trained to understand and use money. America did not teach him the language of the great ideals, just as England did not teach it to Dickens and Thackeray. Consequently, though nobody can suspect Dickens or Mark Twain of lacking the qualities and impulses that are the soul of such grotesque makeshift bodies as Church and State, Chivalry, Classicism, Art, Gentility, and the Holy Roman Empire; and nobody blames them for seeing that these bodies were mostly so decomposed as to have become intolerable nuisances, you have only to compare them with Carlyle and Ruskin, or with Euripides and

---

[3]Twain had published an ironic "defence" of General Frederick Funston (1865–1917), who in 1901, in the Spanish-American War, had "treacherously" captured the Filipino insurrectionist Emilio Aguinaldo.

[4]The correct title of Twain's novel is *A Connecticut Yankee in King Arthur's Court*.

[5]James ("The Admirable") Crichton (1560–85?) was a legendary scholar who disputed doctrines of the Thomists and Scotists. A noted swordsman, he died in a brawl at Mantua.

[6]John D. Rockefeller (1839–1937), celebrated American millionaire, was founder and head of the Standard Oil Company.

Aristophanes, to see how, for want of a language of art and a body of philosophy, they were so much more interested in the fun and pathos of personal adventure than in the comedy and tragedy of human destiny.

The Dickensian Strand

Extract from an unsigned program note for *The Doctor's Dilemma*, Wallack's Theatre, New York, 26 March 1915.

As the drama relapses from the Elizabethan summit the elements separate again, and we have serious interest and comic relief kept quite distant. This continues until the Victorian summit is attained by Ibsen, for whose procedure the rather desperate classification of tragi-comedy had to be invented.

The Doctor's Dilemma is a post-Ibsen play, and in it accordingly we find that the scenes have a double and even treble or quadruple character, defying all classification. What is more, the intertwined strands in it are the old English strands, instead of the much less extremely contrasted German or Danish strands of Norwegian literature. The characteristic of the old English strands is their accentuation to the point of extravagance and caricature; so that English writers have always seemed boisterous and barbarous to the Latin nations. Now the author of *The Doctor's Dilemma* was nursed on Dickens, who carried this national extravagance to downright ecstasy, through his delightful gift of burlesquing a character to the very verge of hilarious insanity without ever losing his grip of its reality; so that though nobody ever heard a human being say the things that Dickens's characters say or saw one do the things they do, everybody recognizes in them familiar persons, made more real than reality and more vivid than life.

Naturally, in this English style tragedy is more remote from comedy than in any other, because in it tragedy condescends to exploit sentimental and romantic pathos to the extent of being frequently maudlin, whilst English comedy, being almost indecently free from classical snobbishness, indulges in farce, burlesque and even harlequinade without scruple. In this unrestrained art, accordingly, the amalgamation of tragedy and comedy into a single effect of manifold life takes us further from the stage convention of watertight compartments for each than it would in the more disciplined French school, which has so strongly influenced our older dramatic critics. In *The Doctor's Dilemma* the method of portraying the doctor sails far closer to the wind of burlesque, and of the newspaper reporter to that of farce, than in a French play of equal rank; and the presence of the doctors and the reporter in the most tragic scene in the play is all the more disconcerting to those who like their dramatic goods in separate parcels, however cunningly each effect is made to heighten its opposite. By this it is not implied that the portraiture is false or even caricatured. No one will say that the English portraiture of Dickens is Flaubert or Maupassant. But the method is quite different; and the method of the author of *The Doctor's Dilemma*, though he has been deeply influenced by a continental culture which never touched Dickens, is nevertheless unmistakably the English method as inherited from Dickens.

The Case against Chesterton

Extract from a review-article on Julius West's *G. K. Chesterton: A Critical Study*. *New Statesman* (London), 13 May 1916.

Take ... the children of the poor. Mr. Chesterton is, to his honour, a sound Dickensian, and does not think any child ought to be like Jo in *Bleak House*. Well, the practical alternative, until poverty is abolished, is to spend money enough on Jo to bring him up decently. Who is to have the spending of that money and the responsibility for Jo? Clearly, answers the feeling heart, Jo's mother. Now that may solve the problem for Jo A (pardon the official classification), whose mother is a mother in a thousand, or, to be roughly accurate, one of from 25 to 33 per cent. of our impecunious motherhood. But Jo B has no mother. Jo C has a mother who can be trusted with the money if she is inspected a little. Jo D has a gloriously drunken mother who will not only drink Jo's endowment but force him to add to it as a thief, and force his sister to add to it as a child-prostitute. It is no use shrieking that this is a libel on motherhood. If the thistle of poverty bore nothing but grapes we should not want to uproot it. The objection to poverty is precisely that it inevitably produces such results. What would Mr. Chesterton do with Jo C and Jo D? Will he say, like the bold bishop, that he had rather see Jo free (as in *Bleak House*) than inspected or torn from his mother's arms? Not without denying his master, Dickens, who was always himself Honeythundering at "my lords and gentlemen and right honourables and wrong honourables of every degree" to officiously make Jo their business; to demolish Tom-All-Alone's; to endow and inspect and clean up; and to replace Mrs. Pardiggle and Bumble and Gradgrind, not by beer and jollity and the fighting part of knight-errantry and mediæval religion, but by the sworn enemy and vowed destroyer of the accursed Poor Law: in short, by Mrs. Sidney Webb.[1] He no sooner showed how Mrs. Pardiggle, fool and snob and self-elected irresponsible uninspected inspector, made the miserable savages she inspected worse, than he went on to show how the two decent ladies she brought with her made them better. The bond of sympathy between Mr. Sidney Webb and myself is that we were both brought up on *Little Dorrit*. No use coming Dickens over us. What would Mr. Chesterton do with Jo? His reply would make an excellent subject for an article in the *New Witness*[2] . . .

---

[1] Beatrice Webb (1858–1943) founded in 1909 the National Committee for the Break-Up of the Poor Law. Her husband was Sidney Webb.
[2] Founded (1912) and edited by G. K. Chesterton's brother Cecil.

Is Dickens "A Washout"?

Contribution to a symposium. *Strand Magazine* (London), November 1918.

Mont Blanc is a "washout" for anyone who has barely enough wind to climb Primrose Hill. Don't trouble about the "authorities": try the booksellers.

Ruskin, Dickens, and Shaw as Democrats

Extract from a lecture *Ruskin's Politics*, delivered at the Ruskin Centenary Exhibition, London, 21 November 1919. Published by the Ruskin Centenary Council, 1921.

Now, since Ruskin's contemporaries neglected him politically because they found the plain meaning of his words incredible, I put the question whether in the course of time there has developed any living political activity on behalf of which you might enlist Ruskin if he were living at the present time. It goes without saying, of course, that he was a Communist. He was quite clear as to that. But now comes the question, What was his attitude towards Democracy? Well, it was another example of the law that no really great man is ever a democrat in the vulgar sense, by which I mean that sense in which Democracy is identified with our modern electoral system and our system of voting. Ruskin never gave one moment's quarter to all that. He set no store by it whatever, any more than his famous contemporary, Charles Dickens—in his own particular department the most gifted English writer since Shakespear, and resembling Ruskin in being dominated by a social conscience. Dickens was supposed to be an extremely popular person, always on the side of the people against the ruling class, whereas Ruskin might, as a comparatively rich university man, have been expected to be on the other side. Yet Dickens gives no more quarter to Democracy than Ruskin. He begins by unmasking mere superficial abuses like the Court of Chancery and imprisonment for debt, imagining them to be fundamental abuses. Then, suddenly discovering that it is the whole framework of society that is wrong, he writes *Hard Times*, and after that becomes a prophet as well as a storyteller. You must not imagine that prophets are a dead race, who died with Habakkuk and Joel. The prophets are always with us. We have some of them in this room at the present time.[1] But Dickens the prophet is never Dickens the Democrat. Take any book of his in which he plays his peculiar trick of putting before you some shameful social abuse, and then asking what is to be done about it! Does he in any single instance say: "You workingmen who have the majority of votes: what are you going to do about it?" He never does. He always appeals to the aristocracy. He says: "Your Majesty, my lords and gentlemen, right honorables and wrong honorables of every degree: what have you to say to this?" When he introduces a workingman, he may make that workingman complain bitterly that society is all wrong; but when the plutocrats turn round on that man and say to him, "Oh, you think yourself very clever. What would you do? You complain about everything. What would you do to set things right?" he makes the workingman say, "It is not for the like of me to say. It is the business of people who have the power and the knowledge to understand these things, and take it on themselves to right them." That is the attitude of Dickens, and the attitude of Ruskin, and that really is my attitude as well. The people at large are occupied with their own special jobs, and the reconstruction of society is a very special job indeed. To tell the people to make their own laws is to mock them just as I should mock you if I said, "Gentlemen: you are the people: write your own plays." The people are the judges of the laws and of plays, but they can never be the makers of them.

Thus Ruskin, like Dickens, understood that the reconstruction of society must be the work of an energetic and conscientious minority. Both of them knew that the government of a country is always the work of a minority, energetic, possibly conscientious,

---

[1]Shaw here indicated the presence in the audience of Dr. William Ralph Inge, the Dean of St. Paul's.

possibly the reverse, too often a merely predatory minority which produces an illusion of conscientiousness by setting up a convention that what they want for their own advantage is for the good of society. They pay very clever people to prove it, and the clever people argue themselves into believing it.

Tolstoy, Dickens, and the Evolution of Tragicomedy

Extracts from a lecture "Tolstoy as Dramatist," delivered at the Tolstoy Commemoration meeting on 30 November 1920. Published as "Tolstoy: Tragedian or Comedian?", *London Mercury* and *Hearst's* (New York), May 1921.

Was Tolstoy tragedian or comedian? The popular definition of tragedy is heavy drama in which everyone is killed in the last act, comedy being light drama in which everyone is married in the last act. The classical definition is, of tragedy, drama that purges the soul by pity and terror, and, of comedy, drama that chastens morals by ridicule. . . .

We must therefore recognise and examine a third variety of drama. It begins as tragedy with scraps of fun in it, like *Macbeth*, and ends as comedy without mirth in it, the place of mirth being taken by a more or less bitter and critical irony. We do not call the result melodrama, because that term has come to mean drama in which crude emotions are helped to expression by musical accompaniment. Besides, there is at first no true new species: the incongruous elements do not combine: there is simply frank juxtaposition of fun with terror in tragedy and of gravity with levity in comedy. You have *Macbeth*; and you have *Le Misanthrope, Le Festin de Pierre, All's Well That Ends Well, Troilus and Cressida*: all of them, from the Aristotelian and Voltairean point of view, neither fish, fowl, nor good red herring.

When the censorship killed serious drama in England, and the dramatists had to express themselves in novels, the mixture became more lawless than ever: it was practised by Fielding and culminated in Dickens, whose extravagances would have been severely curbed if he had had to submit his Micawbers and Mrs. Wilfers to the test of representation on the stage, when it would have been discovered at once that their parts are mere repetitions of the same joke, and have none of that faculty of developing and advancing matters which constitutes stage action. Dickens would have been forced to make something better than Aunt Sallies of them. Since Dickens one can think of no great writer who has produced the same salad of comedy and tragedy except Anatole France. He remains incorrigible: even in his most earnest attempts to observe the modesties of nature and the proprieties of art in his autobiographical *Le Petit Pierre* he breaks down and launches into chapters of wild harlequinade (think of the servant Radegond and the Chaplinesque invention of Simon of Nantua and the *papegai*) and then returns ashamed and sobered to the true story of his life, knowing that he has lost every right to appear before the Judgment Seat with *Le Petit Pierre* in his hand as the truth, the whole truth, and nothing but the truth, so help him Rousseau. On his comic side Anatole France is Dickens's French double, disguised by culture. In one of his earliest stories,[1] *Jocaste*, the heroine's father is a more perfect Dickens comic personage than Dickens himself ever succeeded in putting on paper.

After Dickens, comedy completed its development into the new species, which has been called tragi-comedy when any attempt has been made to define it. Tragedy itself never developed: it was simple, sublime, and overwhelming from the first: it either failed and was not tragedy at all or else it got there so utterly that no need was felt for going any further. . . .

Tolstoy is now easily classed as a tragi-comedian, pending the invention of a better term. Of all the dramatic poets he has the most withering touch when he wants to destroy. His novels show this over and over again. A man enters a house where someone lies dead. There is no moralizing, no overt irony: Tolstoy, with the simplicity he affects so well, just tells you that the undertaker has left the coffin lid propped against the wall in the entrance hall, and

---

[1] *Jocaste et le chat maigre* (Paris, 1879) was Anatole France's first published work of fiction.

that the visitor goes into the drawing-room and sits down on a *pouf*. Instantly the mockery and folly of our funeral pomps and cemetery sentimentalities laugh in our faces. A judge goes into court to set himself up as divine justice and send his fellow-creatures to the gallows. Tolstoy does not improve the occasion or allow his brow to contract or his eye to twinkle; but he mentions that before the judge leaves his room he goes through a few gymnastic exercises. Instantly that judge is in the mud with his ermine and scarlet making him and all judges unspeakably ridiculous. Dickens makes us laugh by describing how the handle of the Orfling's corkscrew comes off and hits her on the chin. We applaud the wanton humorist; but the Orfling is none the worse five minutes later. Tolstoy could slay a soul with a corkscrew without letting you know either that he was a humorist or that you are laughing.

Glossary of Dickens Characters
Key to Abbreviations

BH   *Bleak House* (1852–3)

BR   *Barnaby Rudge* (1841)

D&S   *Dombey and Son* (1846–8)

DC   *David Copperfield* (1849–50)

GE   *Great Expectations* (1860–1)

HT   *Hard Times* (1854)

LD   *Little Dorrit* (1855–7)

MC   *The Life and Adventures of Martin Chuzzlewit* (1843–4)

MED   *The Mystery of Edwin Drood* (1870)

NN   *The Life and Adventures of Nicholas Nickleby* (1838–9)

OCS   *The Old Curiosity Shop* (1840–1)

OMF   *Our Mutual Friend* (1864–5)

OT   *Oliver Twist* (1837–8)

PP   *The Posthumous Papers of the Pickwick Club* (1836–7)

TTC   *A Tale of Two Cities* (1859)

Glossary of
Dickens Characters

Allen, Arabella [PP] Ben Allen's pretty sister, secretly married to Winkle.

Allen, Ben [PP] Fellow medical student and drinking companion of Bob Sawyer.

Artful Dodger, the (aka Jack Dawkins) [OT] Boy pickpocket in Fagin's gang.

Bar [LD] Withering satirical portrait of the English lawyer, who knows "all about the gullibility and knavery of people."

Bardell, Mrs. [PP] Pickwick's landlady, with a genius for cookery, who is induced to sue her boarder for breach of promise.

Barnacle, Tite [LD] A pompous senior bureaucrat of the Circumlocution Office and resident of a "small airless" house in the fashionable yet squalid Mews Street, Grosvenor Square.

Barnacles, the [LD] The countless minions and administrators of the Circumlocution Office, practitioners of the art of How Not to Do It.

Bazzard [MED] The lawyer Mr. Grewgious's gloomy and mysterious clerk.

Bishop [LD] Magnate of the church, guest of the Merdles.

Blackpool, Stephen [HT] A much-aggrieved weaver in Bounderby's mill, who is in love with co-worker Rachel but bound to an alcoholic wife.

Boffin, "Noddy" [OMF] The Golden Dustman, confidential servant to old John Harmon, who inherits the latter's fortune in dust mounds upon the supposed death of John, Jr., and pretends to be a miser.

Boffin, Mrs. [OMF] Benevolent wife of the Golden Dustman and friend to Bella Wilfer, young John Harmon's intended bride.

Boldwig, Captain [PP] A man of property in Dingley Dell, who removes a dozing Mr. Pickwick to the pound—in a wheelbarrow.

Bounderby, Josiah [HT] Self-made banker and manufacturer in Coketown—the "Bully of humility."

Bray, Madeline [NN] Nicholas Nickleby's beloved—intended by her ailing father as a wife to his aged creditor Gride.

Brick, Jefferson [MC] A boyish, tobacco-chewing war correspondent of the *New York Rowdy Journal*, whom Martin Chuzzlewit meets in America.

Brickmakers, the [BH] The working poor, living in squalor and ignorance; Jenny, the abused wife of one brickmaker, is befriended by Esther Summerson.

Bucket, Inspector [BH] Intense, sharp-eyed detective, who investigates the murder of the lawyer Tulkinghorn.

Bumble [OT] Pompous beadle of the parish workhouse where Oliver Twist is born, who marries the workhouse matron, Mrs. Corney, but is eventually removed from his post and ends an inmate himself.

124

Bunsby, Captain Jack [D&S] Friend of Captain Cuttle, a seafarer who is carried off into marriage by Mrs. MacStinger.

Butler, Chief [LD] Mr. Merdle's imposing butler, who—fearful that popular prejudice may affect his position—"resigns the Seal of Office" on learning of his employer's suicide.

Carker, James [D&S] Villainous rascal, head clerk to Dombey, who elopes with Edith Dombey and robs and ruins her husband.

Carstone, Richard [BH] John Jarndyce's ward, who tragically expects to make his fortune from a Chancery suit; secretly married to Ada Clare.

Carton, Sydney [TTC] Dissolute lawyer, who loves Lucie Manette and dies to save his look-alike rival Charles Darnay from the guillotine.

Casby, Christopher [LD] Slum landlord and "Patriarch" of Bleeding Heart Yard; he employs Pancks as a rent collector.

Chadband, the Reverend Mr. [BH] Clergyman-hypocrite who participates in a scheme to blackmail Lady Dedlock.

Chancery prisoner, the [PP] A gaunt, cadaverous man, long dead to society, whose private room in the Fleet Prison is rented by Mr. Pickwick for 20 shillings a week; the man is discharged from his twenty years of confinement by death.

Chicken, the (Game) [D&S] Pugilist who tutors Toots, Dr. Blimber's senior student.

Chivery, John [LD] Laconic turnkey at the Marshalsea, attentive to the needs of the Dorrits; his ambition is "to retain the prison-lock in the family."

Chivery, young John [LD] The delicate, sentimental son of the nonresident turnkey at the Marshalsea prison; he is in love with Amy Dorrit.

Chollops, (Major) Hannibal [MC] Frock-coated, tobacco-spitting American whom Martin Chuzzlewit meets in Eden.

Chuffey [MC] Anthony Chuzzlewit's dusty, weazened old clerk, who discovers Jonas Chuzzlewit's intentions to poison his father, which leads to Anthony's subsequent death of a broken heart.

Chuzzlewit, Martin [MC] The novel's hero, an aspiring architect redeemed from his family's curse of selfishness.

Chuzzlewit, Old Martin [MC] Young Martin's rich, eccentric, and domineering grandfather.

Chuzzlewit cousins [MC] Old Martin, grandson young Martin, and cousin Anthony, who dies of a broken heart on learning of his son Jonas's plan to poison him.

Clare, Ada [BH] John Jarndyce's heir, who marries Richard Carstone.

Claypole, Noah [OT] Apprentice undertaker, who insults the memory of Oliver Twist's dead mother and later enters a life of crime.

Clennam, Arthur [LD] Dickens's hero and grave alter ego, the adopted son of Mrs. Clennam, who returns from half a lifetime spent in the East; following bankruptcy and imprisonment, he marries Amy Dorrit.

Clennam, Mrs. [LD] Stern, puritanical adoptive mother of Arthur Clennam; Arthur relates that he is "the only child of parents who weighed, measured, and priced everything; for whom what could not be weighed, measured, and priced, had no existence."

Clickett ("The Orfling") [DC] The Micawbers' servant, a dark young woman from the workhouse, with a habit of snorting.

Cluppins, Mrs. Betsy [PP] Neighbor of Mrs. Bardell, who testifies on her behalf at Mr. Pickwick's trial.

Coodle and Doodle [BH] Lord Boodle, Lord Coodle and Sir Thomas Doodle are alphabetically-ordered generic names (through Zoodle) for government ministers, in chapters 12 and 16. The rhyme apparently originated from the term "Noodle" (numskull; simpleton), commonly applied to politicians and other officious individuals.

Copperfield, Clara [DC] David's widowed mother, who dies while producing a stillborn child to the harsh stepfather Murdstone.

Copperfield, David [DC] Narrator and hero of the novel, which traces his progress from orphaned child to successful writer.

Creakle, Mr. [DC] Brutish master of Salem House, the school to which David Copperfield is sent.

Crummles, Vincent [NN] Actor-manager of a theatrical company, by whom Nicholas Nickleby and Smike are employed and befriended.

Cruncher, Jerry [TTC] Messenger at Tellson's Bank and a "resurrectionist" by night.

Cuttle, Captain [D&S] One-armed, retired seaman and friend of Solomon Gills, proprietor of an instrument shop known as the Wooden Midshipman.

Dartle, Rosa [DC] Acerbic spinster companion to Mrs. Steerforth, for whose son James she harbors a jealous passion.

Dedlock, Lady [BH] Wife of Sir Leicester and unacknowledged mother by Captain Hawdon (Nemo) of Esther Summerson.

Dedlock, Sir Leicester [BH] Elderly, gout-afflicted baronet and proprietor of Chesney Wold.

"Dismal Jemmy" (Jem Hutley) [PP] A careworn actor, who recounts "The Stroller's Tale"; Arthur Clennam is described by G. B. S. as "one of the Dismal Jemmies of literature."

Dodson and Fogg [PP] Rascally lawyers, who induce Mrs. Bardell to file a breach of promise action against Mr. Pickwick.

Dombey, Mr. [D&S] Proud, rich London businessman, father of Paul and Florence and husband of the late Fanny; he is devastated by young Paul's death.

Dombey, Mrs. Edith [D&S] The second Mrs. Dombey, a beautiful widow who marries Dombey for money and position; her mother is Mrs. Skewton.

Dombey, Florence [D&S] Unwanted daughter of Mr. Dombey by his first wife; she marries Walter Gay and provides refuge for her broken father.

Dombey, Paul [D&S] Only son of Dombey and his first wife Fanny; the boy dies after a term of lessons at Dr. Blimber's school.

Dorrit, Amy [LD] Little Dorrit, Dickens's child of the Marshalsea, dutiful daughter of the imprisoned debtor William Dorrit, who finally marries Arthur Clennam.

Dorrit, Fanny [LD] Self-centered, ambitious dancer, sister of the saintly Amy; she marries Edmund Merdle and abandons her children.

Dorrit, William [LD] "Father of the Marshalsea," imprisoned debtor and father of Amy, Edward, and Fanny; often read as a projection of John Dickens, the novelist's father.

Drummle, Bentley ("The Spider") [GE] Fellow boarder with Pip, he eventually marries Estella, mistreats her, and is killed by a horse that he has beaten.

Em'ly, Little [DC] Niece and adopted daughter of Daniel Peggotty, who is David Copperfield's first love; she is later seduced by Steerforth.

Estella [GE] Pip's beloved tormentor; daughter of the convict Magwitch and Molly, she is raised by Miss Havisham and taught to wreak vengeance on the male sex.

Fat Boy, the [PP] Joe, the Wardles' servant, languid and gluttonous.

Feenix, Cousin [D&S] Aristocratic but boyish cousin of Edith Dombey.

Finches of the Grove [GE] A club of rich young men that Pip and Herbert Pocket join.

Finching, Flora [LD] Diffuse, spoiled, artless, widowed daughter of the Patriarch Casby—formerly loved by Arthur Clennam. See also Mr. F's aunt.

Fledgeby, "Fascination" [OMF] Moneylender for whom the old Jew Riah functions as a front, bearing the unsavory reputation earned by his employer.

Flite, Miss [BH] A little old woman driven mad by a protracted case in the Court of Chancery.

Gamp, Sairey [MC] Nurse, midwife, and gin tippler, whose habit it is to quote an imaginary friend and oracle, Mrs. Harris.

Gargery, Joe [GE] Simple, virtuous blacksmith married to Pip's older sister.

Gargery, Mrs. Joe [GE] Shrewish wife of the blacksmith Joe; and Pip's older sister.

Gay, Walter [D&S] Sol Gills's nephew, who is lost at sea but returns to marry Florence Dombey.

General, Mrs. [LD] A dignified and imposing widow and clergyman's daughter employed as an instructress in gentility to Amy and Fanny Dorrit; she is renowned for her applications of moral varnish to the universe.

George, Trooper [BH] Former soldier, owner of a shooting gallery, son of the Dedlocks' housekeeper, and brother to the ironmaster, Mr.Rouncewell.

Gills, Solomon [D&S] Nautical instrument maker, who goes off in quest of his shipwrecked nephew Walter Gay.

Gowan, Henry [LD] A young, shiftless artist, who marries "Pet" Meagles.

Gowan, Mrs. [LD] Former beauty, widow of a commissioner, and mother of the feckless artist Henry Gowan.

Gradgrind, Louisa [HT] Schoolmaster Thomas Gradgrind's daughter, married to the Coketown capitalist Bounderby.

Gradgrind, Thomas [HT] Former merchant turned schoolmaster, dedicated to the stuffing of young minds with facts.

Grewgious, Hiram [MED] Lawyer of Staple Inn and guardian of Edwin Drood's fiancée Rosa Bud.

Grummer, Daniel [PP] Elderly, top-booted, bottle-nosed Ipswich constable, who arrests Pickwick and Tupman for dueling.

Gummidge, Mrs. [DC] Gloomy old widow who, as housekeeper, lives with the Peggottys in their upturned boat at Yarmouth.

Guppy, William [BH] Law clerk, who is enamored of Esther Summerson and discovers Lady Dedlock's secret.

Guster [BH] Former resident of a workhouse and maid servant to the Snagsbys.

Haggage, Dr. [LD] The alcoholic doctor, a debtor in the Marshalsea prison, who delivers Little Dorrit into the world.

Hamlet's aunt [DC] Black-velveted wife of the icy solicitor Henry Spiker, who reminds David Copperfield of "a near relation of Hamlet—say his aunt."

Haredale, Emma [BR] Lovely niece of the murdered Catholic landowner Reuben Haredale and friend of Dolly Varden, a Protestant; both are kidnapped by an anti-Catholic mob in the 1780 Gordon riots and later marry their rescuers.

Harthouse, James [HT] Gentlemanly wastrel who visits Coketown and attempts to seduce Louisa Gradgrind Bounderby.

Havisham, Miss [GE] Jilted mistress of Satis House, who wears her withered wedding dress and raises the beautiful Estella to take vengeance on men.

Heep, Uriah [DC] Mr. Wickfield's fawningly hypocritical clerk—later his duplicitous partner—whose key to success is "humility."

Hexam, Lizzie [OMF] Daughter of a Thames "waterside character," who is assisted to an education by the lawyer Eugene Wrayburn, whom she later marries and nurses back to health after he has been the victim of an attempted murder.

Higden, Betty [OMF] Poor, old, indomitable child-minder and laundress, who leaves home and dies of exhaustion rather than be consigned to the workhouse.

Hominy, Mrs. [MC] An inflexible literary woman, who meets Martin Chuzzlewit in America.

Honeythunder, the Reverend Luke [MED] Inflammatory philanthropist and guardian of the Ceylonese twins, Neville and Helena Landless.

Jaggers [GE] Dark, burly lawyer employed by Miss Havisham and by the convict Magwitch; noted for his shrewdness and compulsive hand washing.

Jarndyce, John [BH] Esther Summerson's benevolent guardian, who proposes marriage but nobly relinquishes his claim on learning of Esther's love for Allan Woodcourt.

Jasper, John [MED] Opium-addicted choirmaster uncle of Edwin Drood, for whom he professes deep affection. Dickens leads his readers of the unfinished novel to believe that Jasper has murdered Drood.

Jingle, Alfred [PP] Jaunty, impudent, strolling player for whom Mr. Pickwick obtains a passage to Australia.

Jo [BH] The Crossing Sweeper meant to exemplify the hopeless condition of London's uneducated poor.

Jobling, Tony (aka Weevle) [BH] Shabby clerk in Snagsby's firm, also a friend of Guppy.

Jupe, Sissy [HT] Daughter of a clown in Sleary's Circus, she ministers to the troubles of several characters.

Kenge, "Conversation" [BH] Mellow-voiced solicitor in the firm of Kenge and Carboy.

Lammle, Alfred [OMF] Husband of Sophronia Akersham, who like himself marries in the mistaken belief that she is acquiring a fortune.

Larkey Boy, the [D&S] Prize fighter who trounces the Game Chicken.

Lenville, Thomas [NN] A sallow member of Crummles' theatrical company, given to constant applications of stage paint.

Lightwood, Mortimer [OMF] Boffin's solicitor, who eventually discovers that John "Rokesmith" is in fact young John Harmon, heir to the Dust Mounds.

Lupin, Mrs. [MC] Amiable, good-looking widow and jovial landlady of the Blue Dragon near Salisbury, where Martin Chuzzlewit's loyal servant Mark Tapley has been employed.

MacStinger, Mrs. [D&S] Captain Cuttle's landlady, who maintains a matrimonial interest in her tenant.

Magwitch, Abel [GE] Escaped convict, whom Pip meets in the churchyard; transported to Australia, Magwitch earns wealth and becomes Pip's secret benefactor.

Mantalini, Alfred [NN] Extravagant philanderer originally named Muntle, married to a West End dressmaker whom he eventually bankrupts.

"Marchioness, the" [OCS] Nameless, abused servant girl of Sampson Brass, a shady lawyer; rescued, educated, and married by Dick Swiveller, who christens her Sophronia Sphynx.

Maylie, Rose [OT] Beautiful adopted niece of Mrs. Maylie and sister of Oliver Twist's deceased mother; she marries Harry Maylie, who gives up politics for the church.

M'Choakumchild [HT] Teacher in the Gradgrind school, bent on imparting the kind of mind-stuffing he himself had received.

Meagles, Mr. [LD] Good-humored, retired banker, who befriends Clennam and his partner Doyce; father of "Pet" and adoptive parent of "Tattycoram" (Harriet Beadle); concerning his views of the French, a stereotypical Englishman.

"Mealy Potatoes" [DC] Workmate with David Copperfield at Murdstone & Grinby's; his name is bestowed "on account of his complexion, which was pale or mealy."

Merdle, Mr. [LD] Consummate man of enterprise and Member of Parliament endowed with the Midas touch, who commits suicide rather than face the consequences of his thefts and forgeries.

Merdle, Mrs. [LD] The fraudulent financier's wife, a bejeweled "bosom moving in Society" for the purpose of attracting "general admiration."

Micawber, Wilkins [DC] The improvident but perennial optimist with whose family David lodges during his labors at the bottle factory.

Miggs, Miss [BR] Sharp, shrewish maid to Mrs. Varden (herself a Protestant lady of "uncertain temper"), later employed as a turnkey at Bridewell Prison.

Mr. F.'s aunt [LD] Grim, severe, taciturn old woman left to Flora Finching by her late husband—with "a propensity to offer remarks in a deep warning voice, which, being totally uncalled for by anything said by anybody, and traceable to no association of ideas, confounded and terrified the mind."

Molly [GE] Mr. Jaggers's housekeeper, former mistress of the convict Magwitch and mother of Estella.

Monks [OT] Alias of Edward Leeford, Oliver Twist's villainous half-brother, who tries to deprive Oliver of his just inheritance.

Mowcher, Miss [DC] A chatterbox hairdresser and purveyor of cosmetics, honest, goodnatured, and helpful to all.

Murdstone, Edward [DC] Wine merchant, David Copperfield's harsh stepfather, who beats the boy and packs him off to Creakle's boarding school.

Nancy [OT] A still-virtuous woman of the streets, brutally murdered by Bill Sikes.

Nell, Little (Nell Trent) [OCS] Child heroine, wanders the countryside with her grandfather, proprietor of the Old Curiosity Shop and a compulsive gambler, who is fleeing his villainous creditor Quilp; after travels that tax her health, she dies.

Nickleby, Mrs. [NN] Absent-minded, widowed mother of Nicholas and Kate.

Nickleby, Nicholas [NN] Young hero, who struggles to maintain the life and honor of his family.

Nickleby, Ralph [NN] A usurer and miser; uncle to Nicholas, whom he attempts to humble and ruin.

Nupkins, George [PP] Magistrate before whom the Pickwickians are brought at Ipswich.

"Orfling, the": see Clickett.

Orlick, Dolge [GE] Journeyman blacksmith, who attacks his employer's wife, Mrs. Gargery, and becomes Pip's enemy.

Pancks [LD] Casby's scruffy little terrier of a rent collector, who plods and grubs for, but finally exposes, the "Patriarch."

Pardiggle, Mrs. [BH] Philanthropist's wife, who obliges her children to subscribe their mites to various "worthy" causes.

Pecksniff, Seth [MC] Moralizing architect and arch-hypocrite, to whom young Martin Chuzzlewit is apprenticed.

Pecksniff girls, the [MC] Seth Pecksniff's daughters Charity and Mercy (Cherry and Merry), known respectively for acid shrewishness and artless vanity.

Peggotty, (Clara) [DC] David's nurse and friend, who had faithfully served his mother until dismissed by the Murdstones; sister of Daniel.

Peggotty, Daniel [DC] Yarmouth fisherman, who lives in a beached, upturned boat with his niece Little Em'ly (q.v.), Ham, and Mrs. Gummidge.

Peggotty, Ham [DC] Daniel's nephew and adopted son, later drowned attempting to rescue Steerforth.

Pegler, Mrs. [HT] A withered countrywoman, revealed as Bounderby's mother.

Pickwick, Samuel [PP] Retired, middleaged bachelor, founder and general chairman of the Pickwick Club, whose adventures are recounted in Dickens's first novel.

Pickwickians, the [PP] An association founded by Samuel Pickwick, which includes Augustus Snodgrass, Tracy Tupman, and Nathaniel Winkle as Members of the Corresponding Society of the Pickwick Club.

Pinch, Tom [MC] An awkward, simple, virtuous bachelor and quondam clerk to Pecksniff.

Pip (Philip Pirrip, Jr.) [GE] Orphaned hero, raised by Joe Gargery and made into a gentleman by the convict Magwitch's fortune; his love for Estella is frustrated.

Piper, Mrs., and Mrs. Perkins [BH] Curious neighbors to the rag-and-bone dealer Krook, who expires by spontaneous combustion.

Piper, Johnny [BH] Son of Mrs. Piper, who, in giving testimony at the inquest of Mr. Nemo, says that "the child knows not fear and has repeatedly called after [Nemo] close at his eels."

Podsnap, John [OMF] Pompous, self-satisfied businessman, a "brilliant social example" and thus the incarnation of Podsnappery. His young daughter Georgiana is a shy, foolish girl, who undergoes training for entry into "society."

Pugstyles [NN] Gregsbury's constituent, who leads a delegation demanding the M. P.'s resignation.

Raddle, Mary Ann [PP] Fierce, contentious wife of Mr. Raddle; she keeps a boarding house.

Riderhood, Pleasant [OMF] Pawnbroker, the swivel-eyed, ill-favored daughter of the river rat "Rogue"; she marries Venus, a taxidermist.

Riderhood, "Rogue" [OMF] Squint-eyed partner of waterman and corpse-robber Gaffer Hexam; he drowns in the grasp of Bradley Headstone, whom he is blackmailing.

Rigaud [LD] Alias Blandois, alias Lagnier, murderous villain first encountered in a Marseilles prison.

Rouncewell, Mr. [BH] The Ironmaster, son of the Dedlocks' servant, who prospers as an industrialist.

Rouncewell, Mrs. [BH] Servant-housekeeper to the Dedlocks and mother of the Ironmaster and Trooper George.

Sanders, Susannah [*PP*] Fat, heavy-faced companion of Mr. Pickwick's landlady, Mrs. Bardell.

Sapsea, Thomas [*MED*] Auctioneer and mayor, "the purest Jackass in Cloisterham."

Sawyer, Bob [*PP*] Swaggering, roistering medical student and disappointed suitor of Arabella Allen.

Scadder, Zephania [*MC*] Agent of the fraudulent Eden Land Corporation, which entraps young Martin Chuzzlewit in America.

Shropshire, Man from [*BH*] Gridley, a man ruined by a lawsuit in Chancery, whose persistent attempts to address the Lord Chancellor are rebuffed.

Shropshire doctor, the [*GE*] Estella's second husband.

Sikes, Bill [*OT*] Vicious thief, a member of Fagin's gang, who murders his mistress Nancy and is accidentally hanged while making his escape.

Skewton, Mrs. ("Cleopatra") [*D&S*] Vain mother of Edith; urges her to accept Dombey's proposal of marriage.

Skimpole, Harold [*BH*] Ineffectual, would-be artist, a child in matters of money.

Slackbridge [*HT*] Trade union organizer, portrayed by Dickens as a cunning, dishonest demagogue.

Slumkey, the Hon. Samuel [*PP*] Successful parliamentary candidate for the Blues in the Eatanswill elections.

Smallweed, Bartholomew [*BH*] A "monkeyish" friend of Guppy, "so nursed by Law and Equity that he has become a kind of fossil Imp."

Smike [*NN*] Lame, retarded boy abandoned at Dotheboys Hall, befriended by Nicholas Nickleby and found to be the son of Nicholas's Uncle Ralph.

Snagsby, Mr. [*BH*] Cook's Court law stationer, who employs Captain Hawdon, Esther Summerson's natural father, as a copyist.

Smorltork, Count [*PP*] A famous foreigner collecting information for a book on England, a guest at Mrs. Leo Hunter's breakfast in Eatanswill.

Sparkler, Edmund [*LD*] "Not so much a young man as a swelled boy," son of Mrs. Merdle by an earlier marriage to a colonel; he marries Fanny Dorrit and accepts employment in the Circumlocution Office.

Sparsit, Mrs. [*HT*] Housekeeper to the self-made Coketown manufacturer Josiah Bounderby, with her own pretensions to gentility.

Spenlow, Dora [*DC*] David Copperfield's immature, incompetent wife, who dies in childbirth.

Spenlow, Francis [*DC*] Dora's father, partner in the law firm of Spenlow & Jorkins.

Spiker, Mrs. Henry: see Hamlet's aunt.

Spinster aunt: see Rachel Wardle.

Squeers, Wackford [*NN*] Brutish schoolmaster of Dotheboys Hall.

Stareleigh, Mr. Justice [*PP*] Presiding judge at the trial of Bardell vs. Pickwick.

Steerforth, James [*DC*] David's handsome and over-esteemed senior schoolfellow, who seduces Little Em'ly and is later drowned at sea.

Steerforth, Mrs. [*DC*] Proud, austere mother of James.

Stiggins, the Reverend Mr. [*PP*] A drunken, hypocritical preacher, who keeps company with the wife of old Tony Weller.

Stiltstalking, Lord Lancaster [*LD*] A high official in the diplomatic branch of the Circumlocution Office: "This noble Refrigerator had iced several European courts in his time, and had done it with such complete success that the very name of Englishman yet struck cold to the stomachs of foreigners who had the distinguished honor of remembering him, at a distance of a quarter of a century."

Stiltstalking, Tudor [LD] Member of Parliament, reputed to have entered a famous coalition with one of the Barnacle clan.

Stone-throwing boy [MED] Deputy, an urchin employed to stone the sexton Durdles if he is away from home after ten o'clock in the evening.

Summerson, Esther [BH] Heroic, self-sacrificing housekeeper to John Jarndyce, her guardian; Dickens's only female narrator, she is the unacknowledged daughter of Lady Dedlock and Captain Hawdon (Nemo).

Swiveller, Dick [OCS] A shabby clerk, who exposes the villainy of Quilp and befriends a servant girl known as "The Marchioness," whom he educates and finally marries.

Swosser, Captain, RN [BH] Deceased first husband of Mrs. Bayham Badger, "to the loss of whom she has become inured by custom, combined with science—particularly science."

Tappertit, Simon [BR] Youthful revolutionist, gripped by dreams of glory, apprenticed to honest Gabriel Varden, and attracted to his daughter Dolly.

Tigg, Montague [MC] A slinking, shabby-genteel swindler and blackmailer.

Toodle [D&S] A stoker who becomes an engine-driver; husband of little Paul Dombey's "foster-mother."

Toots, Mr. P [D&S] Dr. Blimber's eldest pupil, mentally lamed by excessive grinding at lessons.

Trabb's boy [GE] Audacious assistant to a prosperous old tailor.

Trotter, Job [PP] Alfred Jingle's confidental servant; the only man capable of outsharping Sam Weller.

Trotwood, Betsey [DC] David Copperfield's great-aunt and guardian, eccentric though benevolent.

Tulkinghorn [BH] The Dedlocks' lawyer, shot dead in his chambers after attempting to blackmail Lady Dedlock.

Tupman, Tracy [PP] Amorous, elderly member of the Pickwick Club and Mr. Pickwick's traveling companion.

Twinkleton, Miss [MED] Headmistress of the Nuns' House Seminary for Young Ladies, where Edwin Drood's fiancée Rosa Bud and Helena Landless are pupils.

Twist, Oliver [OT] Born in a workhouse and apprenticed to an undertaker, this orphaned hero is captured by a gang of thieves, but is rescued and adopted by Mr. Brownlow, a benevolent gentleman who establishes the boy's true identity.

Varden, Dolly [BR] An honest locksmith's coquettish daughter, loved by Joe Willet and Simon Tappertit; she is abducted during the Gordon Riots, but is rescued by Joe, whom she marries.

Veneering, Hamilton [OMF] *Nouveau riche* head of a drug firm, who is elected to Parliament from the borough of Pocket Breaches.

Venus, Mr. [OMF] Sallow-faced taxidermist of Clerkenwell, the purchaser of Silas Wegg's amputated leg.

Vholes, Mr. [BH] Stooped, sallow solicitor, who corrupts Richard Carstone, turning him against the benevolent John Jarndyce.

Wade, Miss [LD] A sinister, strong-willed woman, who lures Tattycoram from the Meagles' service.

Wardle, Emily [PP] Daughter of the owner of Manor Farm, Dingley Dell, where the

Pickwickians spend Christmas; she marries the poetic Pickwickian, Augustus Snodgrass.

Wardle, Rachel [PP] Spinster sister of a country squire; aunt to Emily and Isabella Wardle.

Wegg, Silas [OMF] Peg-legged errand-goer and scoundrel, engaged by Noddy Boffin to read and explicate *The Decline and Fall of the Roman Empire*.

Weller, Sam [PP] Samuel Pickwick's faithful, philosophical valet, whose appearance bolstered the success of Dickens's first novel.

Weller, Susan [PP] Second wife of Tony Weller, Senior, who distresses her husband by an infatuation with the Reverend Mr. Stiggins.

Weller, Tony [PP] Stout, red-faced, pipe-smoking coachdriver; father of Sam.

Wickfield, Agnes [DC] The lawyer Wickfield's daughter, later David's bright, efficient, and tranquil second wife.

Wickfield, Mr. [DC] Betsey Trotwood's lawyer and alcoholic father of Agnes, eventually rescued from Uriah Heep's machinations.

Wilfer, Mrs. [OMF] Tall, angular, temperamental wife of "Rumty" Wilfer, a poor clerk to the Veneerings; mother of Bella and Lavinia.

Winkle, Nathaniel [PP] Charter Pickwickian, aspiring sportsman, and one of Mr. Pickwick's traveling companions.

Wopsle, Mr. [GE] Deep-voiced parish clerk, later to become an actor under the name of Mr. Waldengarver.

Wrayburn, Eugene [OMF] Indolent, melancholic lawyer, who is redeemed by marriage to Lizzie Hexam, daughter of the waterman Gaffer.

Index